Education: A Way Ahead

Education: A Way Ahead

MARY WARNOCK

BASIL BLACKWELL · OXFORD

ISBN 0-631-11281-2

British Library Cataloguing in Publication Data

Warnock, Mary
    Education.—(Mainstream book club).
    1. Education
    I. Title   II. Series

Typeset by Malvern Typesetting Services Ltd.
Printed in Great Britain by
Billing and Sons Ltd.
London, Guildford and Worcester

Contents

Introduction

There was a time when education was regarded as a luxury, inevitably confined to a few. We recognize it now as a right, a necessity to which all children are entitled. Education must be provided for children, by law; the law reinforces and confirms our feeling that without education a child is deprived. Children, that is to say, are now held to have educational *needs* which must be satisfied.

Throughout the following chapters, I assume that if there is an agreed need for education, then the state has a duty to provide it. It could be argued, as indeed it was by John Stuart Mill, that the state ought to make education compulsory, but leave provision of education to private enterprise. This view would be unrealistic today. Nevertheless, if it is the duty of the state to provide education, this does not mean that no one else has a right to provide it. If this book seems to be concerned primarily with the maintained system, this is because it is that which, on the whole, needs most to be improved. But many of the arguments and conclusions could be applied just as well to the private sector.

What, then, is an educational need? I aim to consider the question *What is an educational need?* to try to define the needs that children have, and to discuss how these may be satisfied by the schools of the future.

Of course adults too may want education, and may educate themselves; and this is an undisputed benefit. But the law is concerned with the needs of children, and of children at school, and it is their needs that I want to investigate. For although the education of children is compulsory, there is notoriously great controversy about what should be provided.

It is idle to think that any single solution to this problem will be universally accepted. Indeed, it would probably be harmful if there were no more disagreement or diversity. All the same, it is useful to understand what kind of a problem it is, and to consider how our more general systems of value can be reflected in our solutions. How we think schools should be is linked inevitably with how we think things in general should be. One reason why it is important to make decisions about education is that other values and other priorities become clearer as we do so.

Before considering specifically educational needs, some entirely general observations are in order. When one thinks of a need, it is always of a need *relative to some specific end*. Even a man's need for food or sleep is relative to his presumed wish to stay alive. We need nails and hammers so that we can make or mend things, clothes so that we can keep warm or look attractive, houses so that we may live in security and bring up our families. All these goals are ends which we value. We *want* these things, and therefore we need the means of attaining them. Whenever someone says that he needs something it is always proper to ask him what he needs it for, and his answer will specify something which he values.

Educational needs are no exception to this general rule: people need to learn this that or the other in order that they may attain some end which we, or they, think valuable. So in deciding what the educational needs of a child are, we have to decide what valued end he needs education for; to attain *what* do we devise, and pay for, the vast educational machine which now exists.

It is worth making this perhaps obvious point because educationalists often tell us that to ask what education is for is a mistake, indeed a gross misunderstanding. For, they say, education is not *for* anything. It is valuable simply and solely for itself and not for the attainment of any other end. To think that education is for something other than itself is, they say, to confuse education with training, or apprenticeship, which will indeed always be directed to some goal. To perpetrate this confusion, we are told, is greatly to demean education, for it is to suggest that it must be primarily useful.

It is not, as a matter of fact, clear to me why something

useful and necessary should not also be valued for its own sake, or for the pleasure it gives (as food is). But, in any case, if we are concerned with children, and if we are prepared to talk of their educational needs, then we must be prepared to discuss the ends or purposes for which they need to be educated. And since they do not remain children for ever, and are not compulsorily educated beyond the time when they are children, it is reasonable to suppose that the end or purpose has to do with the rest of their lives, with the part of their lives which comes *after* school.

Thus an educational need is a need relative to the future of the child who has it; and our question must be this: What do we value in the whole life of a man for which education while he is a child is necessary? What sort of lives do we want people to be able to lead, which they would not be able to lead without education?

Now first it must be remembered that we ask these questions with regard to children, who, at least when they start on their education, cannot be supposed to have many serious thoughts about their own futures: so it is their parents, and other adult members of society, who have essentially to decide what they want children educated for. I shall return to this point, for it has important political implications. Most parents, if asked what they want for their children, would say that they wanted happiness. Then they might say that they wanted them to be independent, able to live well and to have satisfying and interesting jobs. Then they might say that of course they wanted them to behave well, and live morally respectable as well as happy and independent lives. These obvious desires are of the greatest importance, if we are thinking of the goals of education.

Happiness, as we all know, cannot be ensured. It is partly a matter of temperament, partly a matter of chance. It will not come if too energetically sought. Nevertheless, however vague and ill-defined our notion is, we all want happiness for our children as well as for ourselves; and one major ingredient of happiness is undoubtedly to find things interesting. To put it another way, boredom is the great enemy of happiness. So one of the universal and absolutely legitimate demands which parents make of a school is both that it shall not itself be boring, and, more generally, that it should *lead* to interest, and non-boredom. For it is, it seems to me, an essential part of the goal of education that it should open up to children sources of interest which they could not have had without it. So not only must a school interest its pupils at the time when they are there, but it must also provide them with perennial possible sources of pleasure and enjoyment, in such a way that when they have left school they will want to go on, want to pursue the interests they acquired at school, or the skills they began to learn there. Thus one of the main purposes of education will be fulfilled if a child at school learns to become absorbed in some subject, or to devote himself to some hobby, or to practise some skill in a proper and professional way. Even if that particular skill is forgotten, he will retain the knowledge of what it is like to do something properly, how to find out about things, how to play a game well rather than badly, what a high standard of performance is like, and what demands it makes. All these are things which he can learn at school and take with him when he has left, as equipment for the enjoyment of the rest of his life, and as a source of a continued interest in new possibilities. To exercise his imagination, to learn to look and listen and inquire; these are lessons which, if he has learned them at school, may go far to securing happiness later.

The second goal is independence. Parents want their children to be educated in such a way that they are capable of looking after themselves, of earning their own livings and of making for themselves a good life, without too much reliance on other people's resources. Most schools would now agree that part of their function is to teach a certain degree of self-sufficiency to their pupils (though it must be admitted that many are extremely ineffective in practice). It is increasingly agreed, for example, that all children should not only learn to read and write, but also should be taught some elementary practical skills, such as how to mend a fuse or change an electric plug or drive a car. And more and more is heard of 'citizenship', of learning how to fill up tax forms, understand agreements and contracts of various kinds, or register complaints to appropriate authorities. All these things are conducive to independence, and to a kind of useful understanding of the environment which may well be thought essential to good education.

On the other hand, parents are also anxious that their children have independence of a different kind, for a possible choice of careers, for the possibility of making a good living, sometimes of doing better than they have done themselves. And it is here that parents and educationalists may seem most obviously at odds. For the theorists tend to hold that education must not be geared towards jobs; that such a materialistic 'utilitarian' view is low and degrading, and that the proper function of a school cannot be to 'turn out' products according to the demands of the employment market. Industrialists are especially held to blame for demanding a particular kind of education which, it is suggested, would have the pupils at school disciplined in certain useful skills, but lacking in individuality and creativity, mere 'fodder' for industry itself.

As long as parents had reason to believe that academic excellence and a good 'Arts' degree could lead, in the end, to a good career and the possibility of both money and power, they had perhaps no real or urgent need to dissent from the views of the theorists. The best educationally seemed also to be the best from a practical or worldly point of view. But there is an increasing feeling both that the most pure academic education may no longer exclusively command the best career openings, and that in any case schools have somehow acquired ideals and ambitions which are quite different from those of the rest of the world, and hardly intelligible to them. Careers advice is of course far more widely available than it used to be. But it is one thing to advise, another to adapt the whole outlook of the school in such a way that the advice makes sense. Parents do not demand that their children decide at the age of eleven or twelve what they want to do and then pursue that goal single-mindedly. On the other hand, they and ultimately their children often feel that what they do at school has no bearing on what they will do next; and that, unless they are going to university (and sometimes even then), the last year or two at school is time totally wasted. In short, the mismatch between school and the world seems to have become more flagrant. Part of the true aim of school education has undoubtedly been lost to sight, if pupils, when they leave, feel that school has not helped them in any way to get a job or pursue a career which is suitable for them. To be prepared to some extent for work is one educational need.

Finally, parents will not believe that their children's educational needs have been satisfied if they do not learn at school, in the broadest sense, how to behave. This is perhaps the greatest difficulty of all. Children no doubt need to learn this, but what precisely is it that they are to learn? And how is it to be taught? Schools speak with varying enthusiasm and sincerity of moral education. We hear a great deal about the 'hidden' curriculum of the school, the ethos, the customs, the accepted norms which a child picks up without being specifically taught; and this hidden curriculum, the atmosphere of the school, is undoubtedly a crucial part of education.

Teachers themselves understandably often feel that too much is asked of them if they have to try to remedy what may be a moral blank in the child's learning at home (another, and much more powerful, hidden curriculum). But whether schools like it or not, it remains true that part of a child's educational need is to learn how to think about what is right and what is wrong, how to take into account the rights and wishes of other people, how to adapt himself to the demands and eccentricities of others, how to fulfil obligations, keep promises and carry out responsibilities. A school which did nothing to enable its pupils to learn these things would have partly failed to satisfy their educational needs.

Educational needs, then, exist, and are determined according to what we value in life as a whole. To make such an evaluation, to draw up a list of priorities, might be a private exercise for every individual. The questions involved might be personal or moral questions, but in the case of education a public policy has to be adopted, and public money spent on the implementation of the policy. Education has to be publicly provided. And thus the question of what values are presupposed in a system of education becomes inevitably a matter of politics, not of morals or of taste.

For if the state is to supply education, what sort of education is it going to supply? To whom? And for how long? These and other related questions are quite manifestly political, such as any political party must consider, and on which it must make its policy known. Thus the notion that politics might be kept out of education is absurd. It would be possible only if educational goals could be determined absolutely separately from any other goals, or if the values presupposed in education were totally different from the values of society as a whole. But we have seen that this is not so.

Two things follow: the government in power for the time being has to exercise decisive and paternalistic control to get the schools that it wants. However much is left to local authorities or to non-political bodies such as the Schools Council, ultimately decisions have to be made by the Secretary of State. Obviously not every educational decision will be directly attributable to government; nor will party politics necessarily involve constant changes in educational policy, or so one may hope. But the fact is that the allocation of resources, the decision to close or not to close particular educational establishments, giving local authorities the duties of organizing their schools and allocating pupils in one way or another . . . all such decisions are manifestly political, and they reflect a particular set of values. Moreover, they exercise a profound effect on the nature of the actual education provided for children at school. It is no use to pretend that this need not be so. Someone has to make such decisions. A certain amount of paternalism and dictation from above is totally unavoidable.

But precisely because the questions at issue are political, all of us are, mercifully, entitled to air our views, and to use every local or national means at our disposal to make known what we, members of society, want. If education were outside politics it might properly be considered a matter only for experts. Since it is political, there are overriding reasons why experts alone should not determine educational policy, and it becomes a matter of supreme importance that society, and above all the parents of children who are being

Mary Warnock

educated, should have the issues clearly presented to them, and should make known what they want. Democracy is a form of political institution; and we should not forget that though teachers and other experts have a right to be heard on matters of detail, on the general issues of value involved there are no experts. We must make our political evaluations for ourselves.

There is another reason, however, for saying that politics cannot be kept out of education. The concept of equality has come to have a unique and dominating role in political thought, not so much perhaps in theoretical or academic thought as in the thought lying immediately behind practical politics. (Liberty and fraternity seem to have become mere consequential dependants upon equality, the acknowledged leader of the trio.) Equality of educational opportunity, equality in the distribution of education, in the abolition of selection, integration, the removal of élitism, all these are potent political ideas. The difficulty is that none is clear, and all are easily misunderstood.

In the following chapters these concepts inevitably appear. For the concept of equality has dominated, perhaps bedevilled, educational as well as more general political thought for the last thirty years. In the 1940s, equality of *educational opportunity* was believed to be an overriding and thoroughly estimable aim. For education, and those powerful positions in the world held to follow upon education, were thought of as matters of competition. Not everyone could win, but at least everyone ought to have a fair and equal chance to enter the competition, and this, it was believed, could be brought about by the eleven-plus examination.

But two things went wrong. First, the eleven-plus itself became suspect as a means of selection. It did not always select the right people. In particular it selected too many of the middle classes. Secondly, it became clear that a mere chance to enter the lists to be selected was not enough. Those children who were not selected for grammar school did not, realistically, get any further chances at all, or so it was believed. Just one educational opportunity was a cruel farce. So what was demanded next was not equality of opportunity, but something like *equality of education*. Hence the comprehensive school, which began as a convenient and often satisfactory way of educating very different children under the same roof, became identified with a demand to give all children the very same education, so that neither their social nor their intellectual differences should distinguish them one from another. The school as an instrument of social engineering was the dominant thought of much of the planning of the sixties and early seventies.

But things have changed. The years 1976 and 1977, while marked by no great educational reforms, still less revolutions, brought into the open what should have been obvious long before, that other values than that of equality were crucial if our society was to get the educational system it actually wanted. It is hard to accept, but nevertheless true, that people have many different ideals and values; each person, that is, values a number of different things, and not all of these values are compatible with one another. In ordinary life we are perfectly familiar with this fact, and we make all kinds of compromises which allow us to have some of all the things we value; some company and some solitude, some time to listen to music, some time to work, some time to talk to our friends; a certain amount of money spent on drink, some on the garden, and so on. No one believes that if you like going for holidays, you have to like it to the exclusion of everything else, nor even that if you believe in truthfulness, you must always prefer truthfulness to charity. So it is in politics. Equality is indeed a value, but it is not the only value. There are other desirable public goods, other things which we may want everybody to have, which are not strictly compatible with equality, or which at least a pursuit of equality does not ensure. Once this is recognized, then it is time to turn our attention to those other goods, and consider them, attempting to weigh up just how important we believe them to be.

And it seems clear that if we think of the provision of education as a matter of satisfying needs, then the idea of equality is not enough to determine what education should be like. For though our aims for all children may, in the broadest terms be the same, though we may want for all of them that imaginative enjoyment of their lives and that independence discussed above, yet what they need in order to achieve such goals may differ vastly. A musically talented child cannot achieve the goal of imaginative satisfaction, creativity and enjoyment unless he has music lessons of a high standard. A deaf child cannot achieve his possible fulfilment unless he is taught language, elaborately and painstakingly, at an early age. It was the concept of educational need which first compelled us to consider the values presupposed by education. But it is manifest that all needs are not the same. So it is time to turn to the consideration of particular needs, and to the consequences which their satisfaction may have for the educational system as a whole.

1

Early Childhood

It is the duty of local authorities to provide education for all children from the age of five until the age of sixteen. After age sixteen, some children will have their education paid for, others will not, and many will have no education at all. The same is true in the case of education before age five. The notion of education is closely related in people's minds with that of school. Thus there is a circular argument: since compulsory school starts at five, it often seems that whatever goes on before that age cannot properly be called education, even though it would be acknowledged by everyone that children do a great deal of learning between birth and five years.

I should be the first to agree that not all learning is a matter of education. It is to be hoped, that is, that all men and women go on learning throughout life, but we would not aspire to having them all *educated* throughout their lives. Similarly, there is a great deal that children learn, especially the immensely subtle and complicated business of speech in their native language, which they just pick up, and which it would hardly be true to say that they were taught. Thus to speak of education in such a context may seem absurd.

It is this kind of consideration that makes discussion of preschool education difficult and complicated. There is a great difficulty in pressing for more preschool provision. At present, preschool provision is not a matter of statutory duty; and therefore in a time of financial stringency it is very natural that local authorities should look first at what it is actually their duty to provide, and cut out the rest.

On the other hand, it would be ineffective and probably impossible to lower the age of compulsory education and this for reasons which are not only financial. For in the first place, if four rather than five became the official age for education to begin, this would still leave out a number of children who need educational provision earlier than four, so the new provision would not effectively satisfy the need. Secondly, there is a strong feeling, only partly supported by research evidence, that it is better for children under the age of five to be at home, and taught, if at all, by their parents. And this feeling would certainly make it difficult to get agreement to a lowering of the statutory school attendance age. Therefore if increased provision is needed, it must be argued for on the basis of provision for those children whose parents want it for them, or for those whose *need* for education has been discovered by people other than the parents.

Arguing on this basis, there seems to me to be no doubt whatever of an urgent need for increased provision. It is generally accepted that what a child learns between the age of about eighteen months and five is of crucial importance to his whole future, that every experience he has at this age is a source of learning, and that, above all, if he does not learn his own language during these years, he may be seriously disadvantaged. These considerations are accepted as overwhelming arguments for the very early education of children who have sensory handicaps, especially the deaf. The same arguments apply with equal force (and are increasingly seen to do so) to the education of the severely mentally handicapped. Children with severe learning problems may, if they do not receive early education, end up in institutions, totally incapable of looking after themselves. If they are educated early the quality of their lives may be very little worse than that of many others, and they will, at the very least, be able to enjoy a small measure of independence. The work done in the Hester Adrian Institute in Manchester, among other centres, has amply demonstrated these facts.

But what is true of these handicapped children is also true, though less obviously and dramatically, of many thousands of other children. For there are many different reasons why a child may have a limited range of experience to learn from, or a restricted access to language. Children who are handi-

capped are often said to be those who need to be specifically taught the things which normal children pick up
for themselves. Therefore, it is argued, *education*, actually
being taught things as opposed to just learning them, has to
start earlier and extend more widely into everyday life for
handicapped children than for others. But educational
handicap may arise from factors other than biological ab-
normalities: there are many kinds of deprivation other than
sensory deprivation. Moreover, there is no exact way of
measuring the effect of linguistic impoverishment on subsequent educational performance. Many of those children
who are later categorized as educationally subnormal might
be classified as normal if they had had a chance to learn more
of their own language when they were very young.

For learning a language as a native speaker is not merely
a matter of vocabulary, or of idiom. It is impossible to
separate language from ideas, or the acquisition of language
from forming and understanding concepts. In an article in
the *Lancet* of January 1978 Dr Muir Gray suggested that the
reason for 'the failure of preventative medicine' was linguistic impoverishment, rather than social or financial impoverishment, among those people who most needed health
education. His thesis was that many people have no concept of a future that can be influenced by what they do in
the present. They are conceptually trapped in the present,
and cannot be induced to take measures now which are
aimed only at some future good.

This thesis, taken by itself, may seem exaggerated: it is not
necessarily a matter of efficiency in using or understanding
language which makes some people prepared, for example,
to take out insurance policies, nor is it necessarily a sign of
linguistic deprivation to be feckless. To speak as Dr Gray
does of our 'linguistic framework' as determining how we
behave is perhaps unduly grand a claim. Yet it is undoubtedly through what we *say* that we make real for
ourselves those concepts which we truly understand, including the concept of the future. Again, it is difficult to see
how, without language, one could envisage or describe a
future which might be different from the present. And if this
cannot be clearly envisaged, then it is impossible to initiate

any planned change. So linguistic poverty may well go with a certain kind of resignation, a powerlessness and lack of motivation to set about any kind of improvement.

Less philosophically, it is obvious that a child needs to be able to explore linguistic possibilities by talking with adults. Even a child with no sensory handicaps, and of normal intelligence, may suffer if he is deprived of this stimulus of talking.

There are, therefore, two kinds of children who urgently need nursery education. There are those who manifestly cannot learn from experience without help, or who because of their disabilities, are simply going to be short of experiences, unless these are supplied them by education. Secondly, there are those children who, as a result of a whole range of different circumstances, will be at least linguistically deprived if they do not have nursery education, even though they have no sensory, physical or mental disability. Parents of such children may themselves recognize that their children are likely to be deprived if they do not go to school. Both parents, for example, may work long hours, and their children may be looked after, when they are working, by someone who does not speak English, or does not think of talking much to children. More probably, the parents will not think about this kind of possible language or stimulus-deprivation at all, and in such a case it is to be hoped that someone, perhaps a health visitor or a doctor, may recognize and expose the educational as well as the medical needs of the child.

But what kind of provision should there be for these children? Whether there should be more places in actual nursery schools, or nursery units attached to primary schools, or whether provision should sometimes be part-time, or in organized play groups or day nurseries—these questions seem to suggest various answers, and there is probably no single best form of provision. The crucial thing is that there should be more. Private school classes and groups ought to be actively encouraged, with the help of grants. Those parents who are willing to group together and pay for premises and qualified teachers should be able to do so and encouraged; and local authorities should then take up places in private classes as well as starting or enlarging their own.

There is a large number of people anxious to work, at least part-time, in the field of nursery education; and although it is obviously essential to have professionals working alongside amateurs, the role of the amateur and the volunteer must not be underestimated. Teachers will be very rash to stand so much on their professional dignity that they eliminate all non-professional workers from the classes. For one thing, many of these amateurs are themselves parents, whose knowledge is useful and whose co-operation is essential. Secondly, from a purely self-interested point of view, local authorities are simply not going to employ enough teachers to fill the need. Nursery provision can be increased *only* if the private sector is allowed to grow; and only so will there be an overall increase in the number of jobs for teachers. Co-operation between the paying and the non-paying sectors is perhaps more essential here than in any other area of education.

For there is, it seems to me, no doubt that in spite of the powerful arguments to show that many more children should have education before they are five than are at present receiving it (and in spite of statistics which suggest that we are among the most backward of all European countries in this respect) the provision of nursery education will always come low on the list of local authority or government priority.

It is difficult to put much force or efficacy into an argument for spending more money on something which a large number of people think is wrong. Although nearly everyone would think that some children need nursery education for special reasons, many think that children without special handicaps ought not to have it. They firmly believe that a normal child younger than five belongs in the home, and that a mother's place is in the home as well. Middle class parents, therefore, who either employ someone else to look after their young children or manage to secure places for them at nursery school, or who do both these things, are prone to feelings of guilt.

At present, the most successful argument for more nursery

provision is that some mothers of young children will go out to work and may leave their children with unsatisfactory baby-minders. Therefore it is necessary to provide proper day-nursery facilities for these children, and, later, nursery school. But this is not an educational argument; it is a social argument, based on the supposition that school is the *next best thing* to the child's being able to stay at home with his mother who, selfishly, will not keep him.

It is time that a more positive argument based on the educational value for the future of the child began to be taken seriously. As more research is done on the effectiveness of early learning, early education will begin to seem a more sensible goal. But if social arguments *are* to be used, it is time that these, too, were made more realistic. A mother who decides to work and to send her three- or four-year-old to school is not in fact neglecting her child if he is actually learning, is happy, and not bored, and if he comes home every day to a stable and agreeable home. Not being in the company of his mother all day cannot be held to constitute neglect.

It is essential that women should be in a position to work, to earn, to use their qualifications as freely as men. They should not be told that, if they want to work, they either should not have children, or should wait, and return to work when their children are older. Such advice, given to women so frequently that it has become a kind of unexamined axiom, is based on a psychological theory which has never been, and never could be, empirically proved. It pays no attention whatever to the educational advantages for the child which could derive from nursery education, nor of course to the advantages to the family as a whole and especially the mother, if she continues with her career as soon as possible after her child is born. It is a convenient kind of advice when nursery education is in short supply. But the theory which lies behind it is the very thing which seems to ensure that nursery education always will be in short supply.

What is needed, then, is not so much more money, as a change of heart. With an increase in provision there will, it seems to me, come great educational advantages. Those children who are at present suffering from impoverishment of experiences or of language could be compensated. Other children who may begin to show signs of handicapping conditions of one sort or another will be discovered early, and for children in general, the beginning of compulsory school at five will be an easier and a more enjoyable thing. All these advantages are, educationally speaking, of the greatest importance.

2

Learning at School: a Basic Common Curriculum

In the introduction it was argued that, while the goals of education are the same for all children, children's needs in approaching these goals may differ widely. Two extreme examples were mentioned, of the musically talented and of the deaf child. These assignments can be applied to the special case of early learning: all children should learn from their dawning and varied experience what the world is like, should begin to be able to control it, classify it and describe it by means of language and other skills. But children's educational needs differ at this early stage as much as at any other, according to the opportunities they have to acquire such knowledge and expertise. If for any reason they cannot learn without explicit and deliberate teaching, then they must be taught.

considerations will apply. The education of all children must be directed towards those broadly defined common goals which we identified in the introduction. But how these goals are to be approached may vary according to the capacities and the tastes, the disabilities and the difficulties of the children.

The first question is *what* children must be taught if their educational needs are to be satisfied.

Is a child when he leaves school interested in the world he lives in, and its possibilities? Can he think of things that he wants to do, interests or ideas that he wants to pursue further, skills that he wants to continue to exercise, games he wants to continue to play? These are the first questions we must ask. Secondly, is he prepared for independence? Can he look after himself, can he concentrate on a job under his own impetus, can he read intelligently, communicate effectively with other people, distinguish clearly one concept from another, calculate reasonably fast and accurately? Is he in a position to aim for the kind of work or the kind of continued education that he wants? Lastly, has he a notion of values, both those which society demands and those which he has begun to think out for himself and apply in his own life? Has he learned to adapt his behaviour to the constraints of society? Can he postpone his own desires, on occasion, to those of other people, or defer the prospect of immediate pleasure for himself? Has he learned to take on, and carry out, responsibilities? These are the criteria we can use to judge the school, and the quality of the education offered by it.

If there are, then, such common goals, and such common standards derived from them, it seems reasonable to suppose that there must be a common curriculum for all schools. If the goal is the same for all, does it not follow that the road towards it must also be the same? In my view there is no very simple answer to this question. Indeed the very metaphor contained in the word 'curriculum' may itself be misleading. It may suggest too strongly a path which must be trodden, or a fixed course laid out like an obstacle race.

Nevertheless there is something to be said for the race-course image. There must be *some* things which all children have to learn if they are to approach their goals. And at school, with many other children, each child will not be able to follow exactly his own private path towards the goals. An individual programme for each child is neither possible, nor, as a matter of fact, desirable. For learning the same things as one's neighbour, working beside him at the very same task, is itself a valuable part of education. On the other hand, not all children need learn *all* the same things as all the others, nor is it possible that all should learn in the same way. And this is equally important.

It is perhaps worth pausing to consider why the notion of a common curriculum, even a 'common core', rouses the passions, and causes such furious resistance. There are people who conjure up in their minds a vision of all the children in England and Wales learning the very same things at the same time and from the same textbook. This is of course the Napoleonic bogey which continues to haunt even quite intelligent people when they think of education in France. It is difficult to think of any myth which has died so hard. But it is a myth, even with regard to France; and certainly a common curriculum entails no such terrifying uniformity.

Again there are some who are working in schools who resent the idea of a common curriculum on the grounds that the local education authority and governors and managers of schools are legally responsible for the curriculum, and if they choose to innovate or to experiment in curricular matters they are fully entitled to do so. They know their own schools, and it is for them to see that the children are taught to the best advantage.

Such objectors are right as to their legal responsibility (except that, as the law stands, they are obliged to give religious education. They have no choice over this). But they are wrong to pretend that the law in fact gives them total freedom. There are many constraints on heads and governors (many of whom in fact never think very deeply about the curriculum at all). There are external examinations, demands from places of further education, requirements for entry to all kinds of work; and there are local authority advisers and Her Majesty's Inspectors, who could, if things became too eccentric, step in. Ultimately, the Secretary of State has the duty of seeing that efficient education is provided for all children from the age of five. It would indeed be absurd if central government was not entitled to have any views at all about an area in which such vast sums of money are spent each year.

An important part of the public concern which gave rise to the great debate launched in 1977 was the fear that teachers were taking too much into their own hands in determining what and how children should learn at school. The notorious affair of the William Tyndale school in Islington, which hit the headlines in 1975, was a case in which the curriculum followed by the teachers had drifted further and further from that intended by the local authority and desired by parents. The example is itself of no great national importance; indeed, it has long been forgotten in detail, but it crystallized the public feeling that teachers could, if they chose, totally disregard the wishes of the community in pursuit of their own ideology. It was feared that teachers could use the school and the children in it for their own political ends, and that they could treat themselves as accountable to no one and subject to no authority.

A common curriculum seemed to be part of the solution of this problem. It was generally agreed that education should not be left entirely to the teachers. Current demands for greater access to the schools stem from the same source. If any fears about a common curriculum appear to come entirely from the teachers themselves, they will in future have difficulty in gaining a hearing.

But there is a different kind of objection to a common curriculum which is more insidious and to my mind more dangerous than any likely to stem exclusively from teachers, or from local authorities. This is the objection that the common curriculum most frequently advocated is one which is essentially practical. The people who in the great 1977 debate most frequently demanded such a curriculum were those who said that children must all be equipped with certain basic skills, *so that* they could attain some ends external to school, ends which could be stated in terms of the common expectations of society. In the introductory chapter I suggested such goals, and at least a partially common programme directed towards them. I also argued that you cannot separate the needs of the child at school from his needs after school, nor his needs from the needs of society. He must be fitted to work and live independently in society: society must have him fitted to do the work which it is essential to have done. The two aims interlock since he, the child, is part of society.

I mentioned the opposite, or 'purist' view of education in the introduction. Here I want to consider the purists' case at rather greater length, since they have had such a deep influence on the, often unconscious, presuppositions of many teachers and educationalists.

The purists argue that to propose a common school curriculum *with practical aims in mind* is anti-educational. It would mean turning schools into factories, producing the goods which society happens to demand. Education, it is said, should have no external purpose at all. If it is true education, it is good for its own sake, not for the sake of its consequences; it must be devised and valued for itself. An educated man is a man who can think for himself, who has read and enjoyed some of the great works of literature, and whose mind has been cultivated. To regard school as a place to learn some things as an aid to getting on to the next stage of your life is to confuse education with training. Vocational training is indeed useful and necessary, but it must be kept as a separate concept. Education, properly so called, is a different and superior thing. Its aim must be to open the doors to a cultural inheritance. It is this which we must offer to our children if we are to fulfil the duty laid on us by the 1944 Education Act.

This kind of objection to a common curriculum is, in effect, an objection to a particular kind of common curriculum, dictated by the needs of society. It is an objection to the view that all schools should teach the things demanded by employers and institutions of further education, because they are demanded. Such objectors obviously would not regard it as positively wrong to teach children the basic skills needed by those who are to contribute to society; but they would think it wrong to teach them *for that reason*. The deep feeling lying behind such objections is that education must be justified by an absolute standard. It is a plea for a *liberal* education, and therefore an education *not* suitable for everyone. It is education for free men, not slaves; for the more elevated forms of life, not the workaday or common forms. The argument is that to justify education by an appeal to what society needs is to sell out. Children must be allowed to grow and flourish as individuals. They must not be constrained by some common mould which happens to suit the society within which they live.

According to the purists, to demand a 'common curriculum' is to demand that children must be uniform, biddable, conformist and socially useful. It is a totalitarian view of education. Education becomes a weapon of control. As long as we are free, it is argued, we must hold education apart from all kinds of social intervention. Education must, if anything, be in conflict with society. It must not be its handmaid.

Now this kind of argument against a common and a useful curriculum is attractive, and it therefore must be considered with care, and rejected only with caution. But I believe it must be rejected in the end. For it turns on the assumption that the needs of children and the demands of society can be separated. It also strongly suggests that while some children may be fit only for '*training*', others, the truly free spirits, the élite, must have '*education*'. Indeed it seems to me that the distinction between liberal education and vocational training is actually one of the most harmful distinctions ever drawn, and one which dominated educational thinking, not only in the heyday of the public school, but at the time of the 1944 Act.

For there is a sense in which all education is vocational. But this does not mean that children must be required at the age of twelve or thirteen to make decisions, or have them made, about what exactly they are going to do, and work specifically for this end while they are at school. On the other hand it does mean that all children must be prepared, not only for 'life' but, as I have tried to suggest, a particular kind or quality of life after they leave school. And one aspect of this life will of course be work—different kinds of work, with elements in common. It is for these common elements that the common curriculum must be prepared. I shall come in a moment to the question of how the common curriculum should be constructed. And it will be seen to constitute no threat; for it will be a framework of a curriculum rather than a set of detailed syllabuses.

But there are still two more general points to look at first. For our supposed purist objectors have not finished. What, they will say, of those who cannot work? How can we seriously aim to gear education to a life of work in a time of unemployment, which may turn out to be a chronic condition of society? Ought we not rather to be teaching people to enjoy their leisure? And if so, one of the strongest arguments for a common curriculum collapses. For the most plausible argument for a common curriculum was that it should be *generally useful*. But if education is not even *supposed* to be useful, if it is to be instrumental only for the better enjoyment of leisure pursuits in later life, then children must be allowed to learn what they like, or at least what their teachers think that they will like, and what the teachers can teach with enthusiasm.

This argument (which is frequently put forward) is both depressing and deeply misconceived. If unemployment is really endemic, and I do not deny that it may be, then the competition for what jobs there are will be even more severe than it is now. Schools will therefore have all the greater obligation to their pupils to prepare them to get the jobs that exist. They may, it is true, be preparing them not so much for work as for the competition to work. But the preparation will be the same.

In any case, the concept of work includes more than paid work. If there is less paid work available then there will be all the more unpaid. If I cannot get a job then I will have to turn my hand to making my own clothes, mending my own roof and cultivating my own garden, and this as far as possible to a professional level. Therefore, as much as anyone else, I shall need to be able to read intelligently, to think clearly and understand how to find things out independently, and to work on my own. I shall need as many practical skills as I can master. And if I could not do any kind of work at all, my life would indeed be miserable. So it seems, after all, that a divorce of education from the goal of utility, its separation from the work-ethic, cannot really be supported. The purist view of education, though frequently voiced today, is in fact an out-dated and ultimately a divisive doctrine, suitable for those days when education was something which only a minority could hope for. Let us, therefore, dismiss the purists.

Finally we come to the last overwhelming argument which opponents to the common curriculum may bring out. And trying not to be overwhelmed by it leads us to the very heart of the matter. These new objectors say this: it's all very fine to speak of the demands of society determining what the common curriculum shall contain, but how do we actually know what society does demand? Who represents society? Who is in a position to dictate what is or is not acceptable to the community? Parents demand more access to schools, more seats on governing bodies, so that they may determine what the schools should be teaching, but they will not all speak with one voice. Anyone who has taught in a school knows that, while one parent thinks the school should teach new maths, the next thinks the school should be traditional; while one wants children to study only the set books for English O level, another wants a broad and liberal approach. And so on. It is far better for a school to manage its own affairs than for it to be subject to what can only be the tyranny of the majority, or of the loudest voice.

There is great force in this argument. Consensus is always difficult to reach and nowhere more so than in matters to do with education, where everyone feels he has a right to speak. The common curriculum might turn out to be nothing but a lowest-common-denominator curriculum, within which only the most boring subjects, and the least controversial, could survive.

Yet, though it may be impossible to reach absolutely agreed goals, it does not follow that just *any* goal is acceptable. Values are not wholly relative, nor are there, in fact, as many opinions as there are people. When it comes to practice, as opposed to theory, no one actually believes that any view about what ought to be done is as good as any other. Within the society we live in, we can say, very broadly, what ends are desirable.

We live in, and for the most part want to preserve, a mixed-economy society, part socialist, part capitalist, with a very strong bias towards individual liberty. We think of individuals within this society as motivated by a desire to earn, to work, to improve their own prospects, but also to improve society for others as well as for themselves. Thus the criteria for good education which I have proposed are determined by something very like the bourgeois work-ethic, and at any rate by an ethic of individualism, independence and freedom of thought and imagination. Such criteria will be broadly acceptable to those who, in turn, accept the society we live in. But they will inevitably be rejected by those who wish radically to change that society or overturn it.

There will always be tension between those who wish to

preserve and improve society as it is, and those who want to abandon bourgeois goals and establish entirely new ones. This tension will be felt within education, as much as anywhere in society; and it cannot be avoided. But since it is the duty of government to provide education then it is the duty of government to provide education *of a certain kind*, and directed towards certain definite and stated goals. Until the government of the country is itself committed to total social revolution (and even then only if it has been democratically elected) institutions of education are bound to reflect the values of existing society. Therefore, when government issues guidelines according to which school curricula should be drawn up, it is not illegitimately manipulating children to conform to some approved ideal, nor is it wrongfully imposing an arbitrary ideology on institutions which ought to be ideologically free. On the contrary, it is giving expression to what it believes to be the values of that society it is committed to serving.

But if this picture of the role of government in education is to be realistic; if paternalism is to be as harmless as I have suggested it is, it is absolutely essential that members of society who are not members of government, the electorate, should themselves clarify what they want from education. Everyone has an interest in preserving society. Everyone therefore has an interest in educating children as members of that society. It is necessary for all of us to be prepared to define, defend and if necessary aggressively battle for the values we want to see incorporated in the school curriculum.

In particular, we should be ready to argue for these values at a local level. For whatever central government may do in issuing guidelines to local authorities, in the end it will be the local authorities themselves who will remain responsible for the quality of educational provision in their schools. It is therefore right for any member of the community to find out which councillors are particularly concerned with education and talk to them; to use the local media, such as newspapers and local radio, to express their concern; and in general to get discussion, debate and even agreement among those whom the local authority serves. Only then will it make any realistic sense to talk about 'what society wants'.

With this background in mind, I will now proceed to argue for one version of a common curricular framework. In subsequent chapters, I shall discuss the different choices which should be open to children, so that their differing needs may be satisfied within the framework.

I deliberately speak of a curriculum *framework*, rather than a more specific curriculum; and the metaphor is intended to suggest that there should be certain agreed, broad principles about what is to be taught, some wide divisions between subjects, and a recognition that all of these subjects, so divided, should be covered in some way. But, within the framework, there should be room for diversity and experiment.

However, even the word 'subject' may cause despair among some readers. For the educational left a 'subject-dominated' curriculum is a great evil. (The nervous ones tend to enclose the word 'subject' in apologetic inverted commas.) It is argued that when history is divided from geography, physics from chemistry, algebra from arithmetic, art from music, artificial barriers are being erected which are harmful to the total experience of the child. An integrated curriculum, even a curriculum totally based on 'topics' which may be pursued in widely different contexts, still has many advocates, though not, perhaps, as many as it did ten years ago.

At the root of such thinking is a useful, indeed a necessary, idea, that children's curiosity ought not to be frustrated by the objection that a particular question is irrelevant to the lesson currently being taught. Knowledge, it is argued, is not naturally divided. One thing may lead to another, and may lead in unexpected directions. Subject barriers lead to rigid conservatism in the treatment of the subject areas themselves, and are often used as an excuse by lazy, ignorant or unimaginative teachers.

All this is worth saying. For it is certainly the duty of every teacher to be constantly on the look-out for ways in which a child may come to connect one subject with another, and to see how apparently quite different areas of the curriculum relate to each other. No good teacher has ever been unaware of this duty; indeed it is almost the essential characteristic of a good teacher to open up such windows between one subject and another.

But this does not entail that the very best teacher would be the one who broke down all distinctions between subjects. And to suggest that, if window-opening is good, it would be better to abolish all walls is an absurdity. For within each subject, there is much to be learned for its own sake, and separately. There are, for one thing, foundations without which no further teaching or learning of any kind would be possible. If teachers, or syllabus makers, become obsessed by integration, then teaching numerical techniques, the rudiments of French grammar, or the rough chronology of English history might all be omitted, and this, so far from opening windows, would firmly close doors upon any progress whatever.

Part of the objection to subjects is that they are ossified in the public examination system; and this system is itself often under attack because of its emphasis on learning and remembering *facts*. Thus a subject-dominated curriculum is often identified with a whole method of teaching and learning which places undue value on memorizing facts, rather than on acquiring and using techniques. But such a distinction is often exaggerated. It is true that old-fashioned teaching of history and geography did involve memorizing a number of comparatively isolated statements of fact, dates, distances and so on. Moreover, such a view of education, besides its endearingly peculiar appearance in Alice in Wonderland, is still to some extent reflected in various quiz programmes (such as 'Master Mind') on television. But a child actually needs to have some foundation both in chronology and cartography (if this is not too grand a title for the rough knowledge of how to draw a sketch map of England or Europe or the locality of the school).

In any case, in subjects other than history and geography, the fact/technique distinction is far less clear. A multiplication table is not a fact, but it has to be learned; an ability to pass the time of day in France is not a fact either, but it involves the knowledge of some facts about the French language. 'Stuffing children's heads with facts' is often thought to be some kind of educational crime. But it is quite difficult to analyse and identify the crime, let alone the alternative, and presumably virtuous, mode of behaviour. It is better, therefore, to abandon the search for 'factless' teaching, as well as for a 'subjectless' curriculum, and continue instead to seek an answer to the question we started with: what will satisfy a child's educational needs?

There is no serious disagreement about the main lines of a common curriculum for primary schools. Nor is there anything revolutionary in my proposals. There are eight broad areas to be covered, and I shall list them for the sake of clarity:

(1) Reading
(2) Writing
(3) Calculating
(4) Practical science
(5) Religious education
(6) Physical education
(7) Social/historical/geographical education
(8) Arts

Now it may well be true that for primary schools, the idea of a school day strictly divided into forty-minute periods is too rigid; and the so-called integrated day may have many attractions. Nevertheless, it is convenient to think of a roughly forty-hour week; (eight hours in each of five days) and to consider that these forty hours must be divided between the eight subject-areas, in differing proportions according to the ages of the children concerned. It seems to be better to think in these terms than to plan vaguely for each child to do a bit of mathematics and a bit of reading each day. Unless subject periods are divided and organized, the child is likely to move on too quickly to another, perhaps more appealing, subject area. In consequence very clever quick children may get too little mathematics or reading, because they will stop when they have completed their task, and will be given no more to do, while the slow may doggedly plough on, not getting enough help, but cutting down the time they have to spend on other subjects.

Let us consider in what educational condition a child reared in his primary school on such a curriculum pattern would, if all went well, move on to his secondary school at the age of eleven. He would, in the first place, be a fluent, competent reader, capable both of understanding much of what he reads, and of enjoying it, and who would read voluntarily. He would be able to write in a clear, intelligible style, and to show a reasonable competence in spelling, punctuation and syntax. He would be able to calculate fairly fast, as far as ordinary arithmetical calculation is concerned. He would certainly be able to calculate in a practical way, with money and simple measurements. He would have a basic knowledge of certain aspects of science—perhaps some of the principles of photography, radio and television, and of the internal combustion engine. He would, moreover, know something about his own body and about the plants, birds and animals he might see in his own environment, and about the basic skills of cooking. He would be already familiar with the rudiments of the Christian religion and have knowledge of some Bible stories, and with the course of the Christian year. He would have learned to swim, and to play at least one or two team games. He should have some concept of history, particularly of the historical and social development of the geographical area he lives in, as well as some elementary knowledge of the geographical and social character of the major European countries. Finally he should have learned to sing with other children, and should have had the chance to learn a musical instrument. He should have heard, talked about and helped to perform a wide range of different kinds of music. He should have had ample opportunity to draw, to paint and to make things, and to see a wide variety of works of art and architecture, and have begun to be critical in thinking about it.

It seems a formidable list of accomplishments. But in a really good primary school it should be possible for a child to learn all this and more by the time he is eleven. Above all, a child from such a school comes on to the next stage of his education with his enthusiasm for learning almost at its peak, and with an almost infinite capacity for going further. Of course not all children will leave primary school equally competent. But this does not mean that the aim of primary education must be different for the less competent child. It means only that some children will need more help than others, as their particular difficulties become apparent. No primary school which does not at least try to reach these standards can really be thought to have done what is required.

During the first year of secondary school there should be no change in the curriculum structure, except to include a first foreign language in exchange for some of the reading and writing in English which will have occupied such a large proportion of the primary school timetable. And here we come to the first major necessary change in the educational system. For the method and the goals of language teaching in schools need to be radically reformed. Every child ought, if it is at all possible, to learn a second language, at least to the level of being able to speak it and understand it a little. But not every child will need to be able to write in that language, nor to read works of literature in it.

At present almost all modern language teaching at school is based on the assumption that everyone learning the language *will* want to do all these things. There is therefore an obsessive concern with correct writing of the language; and there is very little practice in speaking, or indeed of understanding the spoken word. This is particularly absurd when, outside school, in language schools for business people, or broadcast courses for holiday-makers, techniques of language teaching are being developed which are both practical and successful. It is not surprising that vast numbers of children give up modern languages as soon as they possibly can; that even those who do not give up, but study a language for virtually the whole of their school lives, nevertheless end up unable to speak or understand a word of it; and finally that many teachers, in despair of being able to teach the language, turn instead to a kind of vague European Studies course for those whom they consider too dim or uninterested to learn.

It is a dismal scene. And it could be changed, if the actual objectives of the language teaching were themselves changed, clearly set out, and pursued in a systematic way. Of course there would be some children who would never learn to speak a second language, because of the profound difficulties they have in learning even one language. It would be appropriate to give these children more of another subject. But most children could learn to speak, even if only a little, and it would be infinitely worth while to teach them.

There will be some children who *will* want to write in the foreign language and to read and enjoy the literature of another country. But for them, too, particular specialist provision should be made, though perhaps not until about their third year at secondary school. Second-year students should have the chance to start a third language, either Latin or a second modern foreign language.

In the mean-time all the other subjects begun at primary school will be continued and added to and increased in complexity. Options will gradually be introduced into the timetable.

For it is at this stage, probably in the second year of secondary school, that the distinction between compulsory and optional subjects must be made. I do not believe that most people want their children to drop subjects early or be thought 'hopeless' at a subject, especially not before the age of about fourteen. I think that there would be general acceptance of a broadly common curriculum for all children up to that age, with certain exceptions, and with the possibility of flexible arrangements for individual needs. For there are children who will want to do more of, let us say, music than art, or the other way round; there are children who will go faster and further in, say, mathematics or languages than their fellows; and it is for such children that options should be available.

Meanwhile the compulsory subjects should, with the addition of a language, continue to be the same as they were at primary school. Gradually, for most pupils there would be less need to teach literacy separately; the ability to read intelligently and to write coherently would be exercised in the course of studying literature or history or geography. But such skills must be exercised, and must therefore be tested.

When I speak of compulsory subjects which form the common school curriculum, I am not envisaging any need for legislation. On the contrary, it seems to me that the best way to ensure that some subjects are taught and taught properly at school is not to legislate but to examine. If children need to have passed an examination or test, then the subjects in which they will be examined will be taught.

Parents, teachers and the children themselves will have an interest in seeing that they are taught.

But not all the subjects which I have listed as compulsory at primary school, and which I believe should still be compulsory at secondary school, are fit subjects for examination. No one should be compelled to be examined in P.E. or religion, in music or in art. Nevertheless it is not absurd to say that such subjects should be taught to everyone. Although there is now no law that requires every school to offer physical education to its pupils, all schools do so, and local authorities see to it that this is done. The local authority advisory service is sufficient to ensure that those subjects which ought to be taught at school are taught, and taught properly.

If there were an agreed list of compulsory areas of teaching, there would be no need for either legislation or universal examination to ensure that the areas were properly covered. Guidelines from the government, and a strengthened advisory and support service within the local authority, would be enough to ensure that the educational needs of all children alike were actually being met in the schools.

Indeed, I believe that the inclusion of any subject as part of the school curriculum by law may be actually damaging to the standard of teaching and learning in that subject, though it is difficult to prove such a thesis. The case of religious education is obviously the only evidence there is, and on this opinion is sharply divided. There are those who say that if R.E. were not legally required it would be dropped; there are others who argue that the law is simply brought into contempt by the practice of having an R.E. slot in the timetable, and almost any kind of subject, or no subject, taught during that statutory hour. There are certainly some schools who have no expert on their staff but who, because of the legal requirement to teach R.E. have to get someone to do it . . . perhaps an underemployed classics teacher, who may bring, not only the law, but the concept of religion into contempt by his teaching.

I am convinced that R.E. ought to be taught in all schools, but that it ought to be taught only by people who like and believe in religion and who know something about it first hand. It is perfectly possible for such people to teach without attempting either to indoctrinate or to convert their pupils, to give an acquaintance with the Bible and the prayer book and a sense of what a powerful force religion can be, both historically and as a source of aesthetic inspiration. Without some such teaching, children are actually deprived of understanding a part of the world they live in. Every school ought to provide this kind of teaching, just as much as it ought to provide teaching of history or of literature. But it is better to have no R.E. at all than to have it taught in a perfunctory, ignorant or cynical way.

It will be noticed that, in discussing the compulsory common school curriculum I have spoken throughout of primary and secondary schools. This has been deliberate, for I hope very much that, in the course of time, middle schools may gradually fade away, their buildings used either for primary or secondary schools, or for quite different purposes. I have never heard an argument which has convinced me that middle schools are intrinsically good institutions (though I am aware that there are many such schools which are good). There is a real danger that the children in middle schools may go on being taught as if they were in primary school, by the methods and with the presumptions proper to primary education, beyond the age at which these are appropriate. They may suffer from lack of formality in teaching at an age when a certain degree of formality is helpful. Still more, they may suffer from the lack, at the age of twelve or thirteen, of teaching by experts who can inspire them with the sense that a subject is vast and complex and offers an unending field of future exploration. There is no substitute for an enthusiastic specialist in the teaching of mathematics, science, history, languages and literature for children of this age. But perhaps most damaging of all, the middle-school system demands that children change schools and move to a new setting in which they are not known, just at the beginning of the most difficult and problematic school years. There they have to start again, hastily begin new subjects, or postpone beginning them until it is almost too late, and in general suffer a disruption of education at the time they can least afford it. There are many children who never really settle at their secondary schools from first to last. No sooner have they got there than the adolescent itch to leave afflicts them. It is hard to conceive of a more wasteful or counterproductive system.

To sum up, then: both in primary and in secondary schools, there should be a common curriculum; it should be the duty of the local authority to ensure that all the elements of this curriculum are being properly taught in its schools, and to employ a strong and expert team of educational advisors to cover all the subject-elements of the curriculum. In this way society at large can be satisfied that, whatever school a child attends, his educational needs have a reasonable chance of being satisfied.

3

The Comprehensive Ideal

It is by *what* they teach that schools must be judged, not *where*, nor even *how*, they teach it. That is the fundamental belief upon which the argument of this book is based; and it is the reason why the last chapter was devoted to a statement of the content of a common curriculum for all children at school.

But it cannot be denied that most of the controversy about education in this country since 1944 has centred on the question of where children should be taught and of how schools, and classes within schools, should be organized. Not only educationalists, but parents too, if asked what was the single most difficult or worrying educational problem would, many of them, immediately answer 'the comprehensive school'. We must try to see, therefore, how the question of comprehensive education relates to the question of what children should be taught at school. We must try to discover whether the ideal of the comprehensive school is compatible with the ideal of determining children's educational needs by reference to the lives they will lead after they have left school, an ideal which will be satisfied only if their life-after-school is satisfactory.

Obviously the two ideals cannot be wholly distinguished. For the most serious argument in favour of comprehensive schools has always been that one cannot tell what an eleven-year-old's future educational needs will be. If you separate children into two categories—grammar school children and modern school children—you will in fact fail to satisfy the needs of a considerable number of children, since the schools in which they find themselves will not be able to offer the range of things which it may turn out that they need to learn. But this argument, simple, persuasive and irrefutable though it is, has become confused and emotionally laden, because it has been found to have such strong political implications. (Nor should we be in the least surprised at this. For all educational arguments, being concerned with values, are, as I have argued earlier, *necessarily* potentially political.)

The grammar school was soon seen as essentially middle-class, privileged, élitist; the modern school, working-class, deprived and inferior. And though all children had the *chance* of a grammar school education, that is, all children might enter the competition at eleven, the reality was that it was predominantly the middle-class children who won the places. Equality of opportunity, which had been a rallying cry, came to seem an empty benefit, if the opportunity was only to compete in a race in which the socially privileged were bound to win.

So, in an effort to put this right, and to move towards a new kind of equality, which would be fairer in its distribution of actual educational benefits, the argument began to shift. It was no longer thought simply that the eleven-plus examination was an inefficient selector, but that selection itself was wrong. Comprehensive schools without selective entry were thought to be necessary if the advantage of the middle-class over the working-class child was to be halted or reversed, and if the potential of working-class children was not to be wasted.

So far, this argument has force: and one may add that, in rural areas, the comprehensive school could be strongly defended on other grounds. It is far more practical to have one school than two, one system of transport than several, if children are to be brought to school from a thinly populated region. The idea of one kind of provision has been broadly accepted, and should be allowed to stand.

But the ideal as so far stated was not the end of the argument. It was thought that within the comprehensive school itself 'élitism' must be banished. And since the unhappy (but irrefutable) connection between the middle classes (or élite) and *academic* precocity had been made, it was naturally the practice of singling out academic rather than other educational need that became the target of the egalitarians. Selection between primary and secondary school was no longer the most important issue. The actual content of the curriculum itself began to come into dispute.

As is usual in such cases, the matter is not simple, nor can right or wrong be judged to be wholly on one side. But there is some hope of picking one's way through the minefield if one is willing repeatedly to come back to the question: what are schools, comprehensive or any other, actually *for*? Is it necessarily true that comprehensive schools will fulfil their function better than other kinds of schools? What are the *other* features that a school must have, besides a comprehensive intake, which will ensure that the educational needs of the children in the school are actually met?

First of all, we must avoid falling into a purely linguistic trap. Non-selective schools are called comprehensive; but this does not by itself entail that *all* children must go to such schools. If the word 'comprehensive' does seem to imply this, then the word ought somehow to be changed. All that *need* be implied by it is that a wide range of ability can be catered for within the school, and a wide range of subjects taught. It does not mean that no children can legitimately be educated in private schools or selective schools or by tutors in their own home, or that a local authority is necessarily wrong to allow individual children to be educated in such schools.

It is sometimes argued that unless *all* children in a particular area are educated at the same school, then that school is not 'fully comprehensive', and since comprehensiveness is thought to be virtuous, then the abolition of all other kinds of schools must be a goal for local authorities and for Parliament. There seems to be an element of scholasticism in such arguments. They are used, for example, by those who hold that all handicapped children, however severe their difficulties and disabilities, must be educated in the 'ordinary' comprehensive school.

Of course the advocates of such radical integration or mainstreaming are not always clear about what they mean by educating someone 'in' an ordinary school. It may be that sometimes the integrationist demand would be satisfied if the child were educated on the same campus as his non-handicapped contemporaries, in a special unit or a special class attached to the school. In this sense, being 'in' the school means merely being subject to the same headmaster as the rest of the school. Sometimes this may work to a pupil's advantage, sometimes to his disadvantage, depending on how much interested a headmaster is in his attachments. But the point here is that it is unduly lexicographical, and perhaps disastrous, to insist that because a school is *called* comprehensive, it must be wrong to send some children to special schools. There is no contradiction between having comprehensive and special schools side by side. There is no principle either of consistency or of equality which is broken by the decision to send a particular child to a non-comprehensive special school, if it is here that he can get the specialist help he needs. No other criterion of choice of school is morally defensible.

The same considerations apply to children who, while not being handicapped, and not suffering from any specific disability, yet have educational needs which cannot be met by ordinary classes in ordinary schools. The meeting of special needs, whether needs for extra music teaching, or special teaching in languages or mathematics, or for special teaching in physical co-ordination or in braille must be the first consideration of local authorities, and they must not have preconceived ideas about *where* it is proper for their children to be educated. Of course there will be problems; of course there will be parents who claim that their children deserve special consideration or extra help, when the local authority thinks differently. But this is a familiar problem for anyone who has ever worked in the field of education, at any level. The essential thing is for those who make the decisions to be confident, articulate in explaining themselves, and wholeheartedly devoted to the children for whom they are responsible. Then, if there are disagreements, at least they will be able to explain the basis on which their decisions were taken, without shame, and without the necessity for uttering manifestly political slogans.

Provided, then, that a system of comprehensive schools does not automatically deprive children of the right, if necessary, to be educated outside that system; and provided that, within the system, regard is given to the needs of children, in the sense outlined in our first chapter, then there is every reason to believe that comprehensive schools are the best we could have. But we must now look in more detail at the variety of needs which children may exhibit at school.

We have suggested a common curriculum framework for all children, a framework which will ensure that at primary school nearly all children will be doing the same things (though not necessarily at the same speed) with a view to their general educational competence (and enthusiasm to go on) when they reach the age of transfer to secondary school. And it was proposed in the last chapter that at least for the first two years after transfer to secondary school there should be no major changes in the common curriculum. However, there was an important exception to that general rule, in the field of modern languages. It is time now to pursue that exception a bit further, to justify it, and to consider in wider terms what is entailed in the way of possible selection and specialization in secondary comprehensive schools.

To start with the problem of modern languages teaching in secondary schools needs little justification. Schools themselves are well aware of the difficulties in this area. For example, Patrick Eavis of Manor Park School, Newcastle-upon-Tyne remarked, 'It's like the Battle of the Somme. Thousands of kids go into it at the start, but by the end there is only a trickle of survivors' (*TES*, 23.6.78). Another headmaster is quoted as saying 'We let them drop it simply because a great number wish to do so'. Universities are acutely aware that while there are still some excellent linguists entering from school, the overall standard is declining, and the numbers getting smaller. At the same time parents and non-educational bodies are ashamed and embarrassed by the apparent inability of British teachers to produce linguists as competent as their European counterparts, at a time when the need for competence is rapidly increasing. Here, then, is an area of secondary education in urgent and agreed need of radical reform.

But there can be no reform unless two principles are jointly acknowledged. The first is that speaking and understanding a foreign language is not a specialist, or an esoteric, or a vastly complicated thing. Most people, at least sixty per cent of all children at school, probably eighty per cent, ought to be able to make *some* headway in achieving the skill, even if at a modest level. Secondly, there will, nevertheless, be some children who cannot manage, whatever techniques of practical teaching may in future be devised. It follows that these children should be excused the compulsory second language part of the curriculum, and given something else instead, probably more time in perfecting the use, both spoken and written, of their own native language; possibly more help in English, if English is not the language they speak at home.

To accept this second principle is to accept the necessity for selection within the school. And this is of the greatest possible importance. Somehow or other teachers have got to be prepared to do this. They must learn not to be seduced by the argument that selection is necessarily unfair, or that children always and only fulfil their teachers' expectations of them, and so to select is to ensure that the selection procedure is correct. The damage which such an argument may do cannot be exaggerated. For if selection is not permitted in this crucial area it will not be permitted anywhere; and if it is not, then there is no hope of improving the performance of the majority of children, nor, therefore, of justifying the system of comprehensive education as a whole. Teachers must overcome their natural abhorrence of selection among children. Their task would be made easier if there were some kind of test of basic competence in English, to be taken by all children during their first term at secondary school (not, probably while they are still at primary school, lest the test should look like a return to the eleven-plus, and lest too much time were spent actively preparing for it in primary school). If there were such an objective test, then children who failed to do well enough in it would be selected for extra help in English, rather than a new language.

There is an additional point to be made. I believe that pupils' enthusiasm, and therefore their ability to make progress in foreign languages would be much increased if schools would encourage them to apply for external tests in languages (perhaps the present Interpreters' Examinations, or a new equivalent) which could be regarded rather in the way the Associated Board Examinations in music, dancing and speech are now regarded. There would be at least three main advantages in such a system. First, the actual standard of speaking and understanding foreign languages would almost certainly much improve. Secondly, pupils would be motivated to go on from one grade to another at their own pace, perhaps independently of school, and certainly regard- less of age. Thirdly, if there were parents or children who thought that the teachers' selection had been unfair or had taken too little account of special circumstances, then a child who was not doing a foreign language at school but doing extra English instead could, in principle, take his graded examination outside 'school, and produce concrete evidence of ability. In this way there could be a protective device against unfair or chancy selection.

It should not be too difficult for an Associated Board of Language Schools to establish a series of graded examina- tions, involving both spoken and written tests (but probably for the most part spoken), which could be taken at Regional Centres, and which would soon gain recognition both in educational circles and, more importantly, in commerce and industry. Such a system of examinations could be self- financing. It would not be a substitute for the teaching of languages in schools, but an addition to it. And though schools could enter their pupils if they wished, as they do now for the other Associated Board examinations, it could be used equally by grown-ups as well as children. Such a scheme would take some time to establish itself. But the sooner it is started the better.

It is only if teachers are prepared to select, and select in the first year of secondary school, that the actual content of the language syllabus at school can be properly constituted. At present, language courses tend to be further and further watered down until they are not really language courses at all. The new syllabus must be useful, efficient and difficult to water down. But it must be emphasized that the process of selection, though it must be rigorous, should not in this case aim to pick out a minority of specially able children. On the contrary, the assumption must be that the vast majority of children can learn a second language in this new practical way. It will be a minority of children with genuine learning difficulties who will not be permitted to start.

Once admitted in this case, the principle of selection itself can be seen to be of the very greatest importance throughout secondary education. In general terms one may say that without such a principle the comprehensive ideal is bound, in the end, to be frustrated. For it will not be accepted by society, nor will employers and universities have any lasting confidence in it. Allow the principle of internal selection, and the ideal may successfully and satisfactorily prevail.

But of course 'selection' is an emotive word. I have used it quite deliberately to mean the distinguishing of children on grounds of ability, since in the case of modern language teaching such a distinction has to be made. And there are other subjects for which the principle is of equal importance. To say this is of course to deny the principle of mixed-ability teaching.

There have been many experiments in recent years to try to assess the relative benefits of mixed-ability and selective teaching, in terms of ultimate examination successes, or other criteria. It is obvious that such experiments are extremely difficult to conduct. There is no doubt too, that, because of the egalitarian doctrines which lie behind the theory, passions both for and against mixed-ability teaching have run high, and consequently the possibility of judging the results fairly has been proportionately low.

Perhaps the tide of fashion is turning slightly against the widespread use of the method. Certainly in the middle of 1978 the inspectorate came out fairly firmly against it: they argued that in 800 schools which they visited, and where some mixed-ability teaching was practised, at least for the first three years in the school, there was a tendency for the teachers to aim at an average or below average level. This showed, they argued, that priority was on the whole being given to social rather than to strictly academic or pedagogic objectives.

There may be a case, social or even academic, for mixed-ability teaching for the first three years of secondary school in English (though, not, obviously, for the disciplined teaching of reading and writing which the least able will need as an alternative to a foreign language), and in history, geography, art and music. For in these subjects children can understand the concepts presented to them at their own level of imagination and intellect. The concepts may be general and shared, but are open to individual interpretation and use, and the work done by each child may reflect his own interpretation (though it is worth repeating that even in such subjects, there are those who need special help before they can grasp the concepts at all, or benefit by the mixed-ability teaching).

But there are other subjects, of which modern languages is a conspicuous example, and mathematics no less important, where mixed-ability teaching is totally out of place, since progress depends upon the introduction and understanding of new concepts, the use, practising and perfecting them before the next step forward can be taken. Moreover, it is of no use to argue that, in such cases, each child should work at his own pace and at his own level of understanding, and go on to the next stage when he is ready. To argue thus is to misunderstand the nature of teaching itself.

For it cannot be too strongly emphasized that new concepts need explanation. Reading about them, even watching well-devised television programmes which introduce them, is not enough. Children are capable of the oddest and most unpredictable difficulties in understanding something new, and essentially they need to be able to ask questions, and get explanations fitted to their own idiosyncratic difficulties. Moreover, no teacher can be sure that a child has understood a new concept unless he has practised its use over a number of examples.

By far the best, and the most economical and the most amusing way of practising is to do it with other people. Every teacher knows that it is difficult to teach Latin, for example, to one child by himself. There is a tendency to move on from one thing to the next too quickly. It may seem today that the pupil has grasped the new syntactical construction, but tomorrow he will have forgotten it, and this simply through lack of time to assimilate it through the questions, the misunderstandings, the mistakes—not only his own, but those of his peers. In a class, a pupil profits from other people's difficulties whether they are the same as his own or different. It is far easier to grasp and retain a lesson which is learned with other people. It is also much more fun. (And this is to say nothing of the beneficial spur of competition.) A child who always has his own 'programme', who works always and only at his own speed, is deprived of both a valuable and an enjoyable educational experience.

It follows from this that not all teaching can be radically mixed-ability teaching. There will be some subjects from which, as we have seen, some children will be excluded on grounds of ability. There are other subjects which must be taught to whole classes, but at different speeds and with different degrees of subtlety. Thus selection is inevitable, and with selection, the 'setting' of pupils.

The concept of 'setting' is indeed of the greatest importance in the organization of the secondary school. It is relevant not only to the idea of selection but also to that of choice. It may be worth a short digression here to justify the notion of setting (as opposed to the more radical and quite different 'streaming') in general terms. The point of setting is that a child may have his own class, with his own possessions, his own class teacher, his familiar pictures on the wall, his class responsibilities, loyalties and friendships, and yet for some part of his time he may work in a partially different group. Socially, and for mixed-ability subjects, he may be with his class. But for other subjects in which mixed-ability teaching is inappropriate, he may go off and work elsewhere. It ought to be absolutely taken for granted, from primary school days onwards, that this will happen. As long as it *is* taken for granted, then the general plan can be extended as far as the resources of the school and the ingenuity of the timetable-makers allow. Thus it may be possible for many children now in special schools to be educated in ordinary schools without being made to feel hopeless or different if they go off for even a large number of their lessons into a different group. The remedial groups which at present exist can thus be amalgamated with special groups, and all the children in them may rejoin their own classes for parts of the day.

Sometimes it may be possible to move from one set to another relatively easily. But this will not always be so, since, for example, a mathematics set of high ability children will move much faster than another set with lower ability members, and it would be hard for a new member to catch up. But the advantage is that it does not matter, from the social point of view, which mathematics set a child is in. And even if he is in a low ability set for all subjects, or almost all, there will still be the advantages of sharing social life and loyalties with children of higher ability. All this is familiar enough. But the system must be extended if a really wide ability range is to be properly catered for in comprehensive schools, and if the evils of indiscriminate mixed-ability teaching are to be avoided.

As to choice of subjects, here again the combination of a permanent class base with a flexible grouping for different subjects is essential. But at what stage should choices, self-selection by pupils themselves rather than selection from above by teachers, be permitted? How early should children be allowed to give subjects up? It is easy enough to talk of a common curriculum and lay down guide-lines for compulsory subjects which everyone must learn. But for how long should they apply? And how many options is it reasonable to expect a school to offer, when the moment of permitted choice has come?

First, let us assume that whatever new form it may take, there will continue to be some public examination of pupils at sixteen plus, and in what may be their last year at school. It is thus reasonable to assume that not all pupils will take the same subjects in this examination, and that whatever subjects they do take will have a two-year syllabus. Thus choices *must* be permitted by the end of the third year at school. But is it to be left entirely to the pupil what subjects he takes in this examination? Or, to put it another way, is he to be allowed to choose just *any* combination of subjects, however 'unbalanced'? Secondly, are there to be any permitted choices *before* the end of the third year, or should the common curriculum occupy all the time of pupils up till then (that is, up to about the age of fourteen)?

There are numbers of inter-related questions here; and it is impossible to give a simple answer, since different principles are involved: the supposed evil of early specialization; the positive alleged desirability of a balanced education, for its own sake; the economic importance of teaching as many people as possible together; the supposed advantages of mixed-ability teaching, and the optimum size of a school (since this is linked with the question of how many choices ought to be open to a child).

To pick one's way among all these principles requires boldness and, as usual, a clear view of the goal, that is, of the point of educating children at all.

We have said that school should prepare children for life after school; we have attempted to identify children's educational needs in the light of the grown-up lives they will lead, and this in turn has led to the laying down of guidelines for a common school curriculum to be followed by everyone as far as they are capable of it, and up to a certain level of competence. But what level of competence is enough has yet to be determined.

While it is essential that a reasonable level should be reached by everyone in literacy, numeracy and practical skills of various kinds, there is also another factor to be borne in mind. Children, just as much as grown-ups, have different tastes and aptitudes. That which fascinates one person will bore another to distraction. That which is easy and fun for one is misery and frustration for another. These are facts which cannot be overlooked. It is futile to pretend that children are in important respects adult, and capable of making responsible choices about their own behaviour and at the same time, to treat them like babies who are incapable of making any decision about what they would like and what they would hate to study at school. While children are very young it is perfectly in order to compel them to learn things they would not choose to learn. They cannot have any serious views at the age of six or even of twelve what will and what will not be useful to them. Moreover they do not actually object to being compelled. If anything, they take it for granted and quite like it. School, though it may be in some ways distasteful to them is, or should be, in other ways, quite restful. They can simply do what they are made to do, without having the troublesome business of choices. It should not be forgotten that for their primary school years and for the first few years of secondary school children are children, and like to be told what to do.

But at adolescence things are different. On the whole, for those in the third, fourth and fifth years at school, everything is suspect. It is possible to get children of this age to do things, if it is plainly necessary and useful to them to do it; they will otherwise do things they are interested in but not the rest. I believe that one of the principles to be used in determining a curriculum for fourteen-, possibly even thirteen-year-olds, is that they should be able to do the things they like. It therefore seems proper to institute a test in the compulsory and examinable subjects, English, mathematics and practical science, as well as the elementary modern foreign language introduced at the first year of secondary school. The regular time for taking this test would be at the end of the third year. But it could be taken earlier. As soon as this test was passed, then the successful child would be able to exercise some choice about what he did. Even before choosing his subjects for his public examination at sixteen, he could, for example, start a second modern language in exchange for, let us say, art or some of his more formal English lessons. He could do more science, perhaps, or less music, as he liked.

This view would not be widely approved. It is thought somehow intrinsically wrong, for example, to allow a thirteen-year-old to choose not to attend class music or art. But why? By the third year in secondary school, a child will most probably have had years of art and music; and though it is tempting for each teacher to think 'what he needs is *me* to teach him, and then his enthusiasm will be fired' such thoughts are often deluded. There is nothing in the world more dispiriting than trying to teach a class which contains a high proportion of people who do not wish to learn; and while one may hope to convert the very young, it is hard to convert the teenager, for whom everything which school offers is in any case tarred with a fatal brush of unreality and irrelevance.

And let no one say that better teachers, smaller classes or more dynamic and child-orientated methods would eliminate this fatal weight of boredom and disaffection. These things may sometimes help. But they cannot cure the age-old ill of adolescence, if ill it be. I am not sure that it would be better if everyone of thirteen, fourteen and fifteen loved school, and wanted to work. The period of detachment, of critical aloofness from whatever is on offer, may well be essential to independence and growth. My plea would be rather to accept the facts, and allow school to continue without too overt an effort to please or to accommodate, while at the same time exercising as little compulsion as possible. Compulsion in youth should be followed by relative freedom later.

If this principle is to be carried out, then it follows that some flexibility will exist for children, even in their third year at secondary school, provided that they succeed in passing the necessary test in their basic subjects. But every school should of course be entitled to its own policy about what is and what is not to remain compulsory. By the beginning of the fourth year, however, whatever policy has been adopted up to that point, decisions have to be taken about what subjects are to be studied for the first external examination (let us continue to call it O level, whatever its real name may be).

Even though there may be only one examination system for sixty per cent or so of all the children in school, still it will be necessary at this stage for teachers to determine who is to take an external examination at all and who is not; and then to try to organize those who are taking examinations into manageable groups. At this stage the brave words about mixed-ability teaching will tend to be less often heard, or so it is hoped. At any rate it is essential that the school should be so organized that pupils can take whatever spread of subjects may leave open for them the greatest range of later choices. It is very likely that a certain degree of balance between the arts and the sciences will increasingly be demanded by universities, and other institutions of higher education, especially for those intending to train as teachers. And obviously since children do not know, in their fourth year at school, what they want to do, the efficient school will guide them to taking a good mix of arts and sciences, with at least one foreign language, in their O level examinations.

But there will be a very large number of pupils in any comprehensive school who will leave school at sixteen, and who would, at the present time, be entered for CSE rather than O level. On the scheme here proposed, these children would be given a test in basic subjects at the end of the third year at school. For those who pass, the choice of examination subjects should be open. For those who do not, work can still go forward in the basic subjects, alongside the newly chosen examination subjects. It seems to me that it would be very foolish to insist on any particular spread of subjects, or to make too much of the theoretical desirability of 'balance', for such pupils. Far more important is to encourage them to pursue whatever interests them, and to allow them to make use of all the resources of school to follow a path of their own choosing, however 'unbalanced', even specialist, that path may be.

Thus it would be far better to allow someone to take public examinations in woodwork, art, technical drawing and metal work, if such a combination were possible, and enjoy the increased skill and specialization thus acquired, than to insist that he must have some subject in his list which made him write essays, or work in the science laboratories, if this was not to his taste. Once again the principle should be 'compulsion for children; freedom for adolescents'. If the basic reading, writing, calculation and elementary science had been learned, and a test in them had been passed, then it seems that there can be nothing wrong in spending the last two years at school pursuing individual interests with the benefit of teaching and the resources of the school, whether these interests are all scientific or all on the arts side, provided that nothing is being overlooked which might be an entrance requirement for employment or further education.

The system of choice of subject will, to some extent, look after the problems of mixed-abilities being taught together. Some subjects, that is, will be chosen only by the potentially academic. But this self-selection will not cover the whole ground. Among those doing, let us say, O level English or O level mathematics there will still be a very wide range of ability, far wider than there is even at present, if CSE and O level are really to be in some sense amalgamated. It will be in such subjects as these then that teachers will have to be bold, and separate children into sets according to ability. Unless a school is prepared to insist on such a policy, and provide both the teachers and the space necessary for the division into sets, then the new, combined examination system is destined to failure, since neither the top nor the bottom of the ability range will be properly catered for.

Perhaps more important even than numbers of teachers, and rooms to teach in (for these may become more plentiful as school rolls become shorter) is the *will* to make such selection. This may indeed be difficult to ensure. For part of the objection to having two systems of examination, CSE and O level, running parallel to each other, was that teachers hated having to decide which pupils should enter which system. But it is idle to pretend that similar decisions will somehow be avoided by running the two examinations together. Whether within the single system there are examination papers at more than one level of difficulty, or whether each paper will have 'starred' questions requiring greater knowledge or understanding than the others, or whether some pupils will be entitled to take a specially set examination, largely set and marked by his own teachers, the standard merely monitored by an external board, it is absolutely inevitable that any examination for so wide a range of ability as the new O level will have to discriminate in its expectations, if the whole examination system is not to come into contempt. And if the examinations themselves must so discriminate, then so must the preparation for the examinations.

It is essential, therefore, that teachers abandon the idea that comprehensive schools *must* treat all their pupils alike. The purely theoretical, even philosophical, point that fairness or justice does not demand that everyone gets the *same*, must be grasped, and acted upon. We must come to believe that the comprehensive ideal is to cater for all children *according to their educational needs*, and that the needs of children at school are partly determined by their measurable and discernible ability. By the time a child has taken the tests in his basic subjects (and indeed probably long before) his ability will be known to his school. Of course there will be difficult borderline cases. But that it is hard to be sure exactly where to draw a line, does not entail that there is no line to be drawn; and it is self-evident in the case of the vast majority on which side of the line they will fall. The merit of the comprehensive school is that where a line is drawn in what turns out to be a mistaken way, it should be possible to rectify the mistake without too much difficulty. So, if a child has been placed in too low a set for his ability, or too high a set, this can be discovered before it is too late to move him. It is only if this is understood that the comprehensive system will at last justify itself.

There is one further question about choices which I wish to raise here. Is it essential that every school in the country offer a full range of subjects at O level? And what about the next stage? Must every comprehensive school have a sixth form (post-O level) so large that a full range of choices is open to pupils then? Once again, the possibility of wide varieties of subjects being available was one of the original arguments in favour of comprehensive schools, and it is still often adduced to explain why comprehensive schools have to be so large. But I believe that the benefits of having a vast range of choices available for children at school has been greatly exaggerated. Of course the basic subjects must be offered in every secondary school, all those subjects to take which in a public examination may be a necessary condition of proceeding to further or higher education at all. But one should not be too much moved by the cries of children (or their parents) who condemn a school because a particular subject or, more often, a particular combination of subjects, is not available. Each school is entitled to its own priorities, and must make the use of its resources which it thinks best. If this means that it is impossible to combine geography with history at O level, or German with art, then it is sad, but not fundamentally destructive of good education. After all, no one can study *all* subjects at school. By choosing some, others are necessarily ruled out. The day has a finite number of hours. It is one thing to look back on school and think 'I wish I had learned German' (or biology or whatever it may be), another to maintain that one's whole life would have been better if one had done so.

Of course there may be special cases in which a pupil has very good reasons for wanting a subject or a combination of subjects not offered at his school. In that situation, he should be able to appeal for help to the local authority to move to a school where the desired combination is possible. It ought to be a matter of concern to a school only if this sort of thing happens too often. Otherwise it seems a good idea for schools within a neighbourhood to specialize to some extent, and to take it perfectly for granted that they will accommodate each other's pupils, especially for A levels, but also, if necessary, for O levels. Changing schools ought not to be a middle-class prerogative.

But if change is not possible, or if there is no available school where the subject or combination is on offer, then this is still not an educational disaster. It is of far more importance to be taught well in a curriculum which is not the one the pupil would have chosen, than to be badly taught in the subjects of his choice. Moreover there is a growing tendency to supplement the list of subjects one can learn at school by holiday courses, especially in languages. There are very few comprehensive schools which offer Greek, for example, but it is increasingly possible to start Greek at the Cheltenham summer course, and proceed to read classics at a university. The ILEA similarly has holiday courses of intensive language studies, often for beginners, and there are other examples. It is not too difficult to learn a subject if one is absolutely determined to do so, even if a school cannot itself provide it. Of course in a world of infinite resources, every comprehensive school would offer every possible choice both at O and at A level to its own pupils. But to do this is in practice impossible, and has always been impossible even for grammar schools. One cannot blame the comprehensive ideal for the limitations of space and of finance.

Academically, then, it seems to me far more important that the resources of the school be devoted to teaching properly over a relatively narrow range of subjects than that wide choice should be introduced for its own sake. And teaching properly involves selecting and setting the pupils in most of those subjects which are on offer. Socially, and in terms of the well-being and success of the pupils, as well as of the general satisfaction of their educational needs, I firmly believe that a school must not be too large. No argument drawn from the necessity of a wide range of subject choice should ever be allowed to justify a school of more than eight or nine hundred, and five or six hundred is better still.

It is often argued that the way to ensure wide choice of subjects at A level, as well as to supply expert teaching, is to institute sixth-form colleges. There are certainly many very good and successful colleges of this kind in existence. But before one accepts the principle, one ought to consider what the ultimate fate of the comprehensive schools will be in those areas where sixth-form colleges have been set up. To denude a school of its sixth form, to have sixteen the leaving age for everyone in the school is bad. Far worse is to deprive it altogether of teachers of the kind who like teaching sixth form specialists for at least part of their time. The effect upon the composition of the staff of comprehensive schools, if all the A-level work is removed, seems to me to be an absolutely unanswerable objection to sixth-form colleges. A system of specialist sixth forms and the recognized likelihood of pupils changing schools at the beginning of their sixth-form years is a far better solution. For if good specialist teachers move away from the comprehensive schools, then the comprehensive ideal will itself be frustrated, and the vast majority of children at school will be cheated of what they deserve.

The comprehensive ideal can and should be defended as the most economical, the fairest and potentially the best and most flexible way of educating most of our children, in a system where education is recognized to have a common goal. But that ideal will be lost if only the least academically interested or the least ambitious teachers will teach in the comprehensive schools. Whatever the other merits of sixth form colleges, their effect of draining away the best teachers from schools is an overwhelming argument against them.

4

The Top Twenty Percent

It is inevitable that comprehensive schools, like all other schools, will vary according to the nature of their intake, the character of their heads, their staff and their neigh-bourhoods. Nothing can prevent altogether the problems of inner-city schools. And there are problems peculiar to rural deprivation as well. It is frequently pointed out that these problems arise out of the nature of society, rather than out of any peculiar characteristics of the schools themselves; and this is doubtless largely true, especially if 'society' is taken to include the teachers, whose attitudes and beliefs, more than anything else, determine the quality of a school. At any rate it is certain that the comprehensive principle itself should not be blamed for the difficulties which schools face, or for the manifest inadequacies of some particular schools. There are sound educational reasons for adopting, and sticking to, the comprehensive principle, provided that, as I have argued, within each school internal selection is taken as a matter of course, and the 'setting' of pupils adopted as a policy throughout the school. It should be remembered that the benefits of comprehensive schools were, and are, supposed to be educational. The principle will founder if it becomes too overtly political, or is too frequently defended on social or egalitarian grounds.

Though in general terms the comprehensive principle should be retained, there nevertheless is one kind of objection to com-prehensive schools now so frequently voiced that it deserves separate treatment. This is the alleged neglect in the schools of what are variously termed 'bright children' or the 'gifted'.

This terminological confusion needs tidying up, before any solutions can be suggested. Who are the children under discussion? Are we talking about a minute percentage of the school population, the mathematicians of genius, or the future solo violinists, or are we talking about all those children who may later go on to higher education? When people talk about the gifted, they often swing uneasily between these radically different senses. It is possible broadly to identify three different groups of children, all of whom are sometimes described as 'gifted'.

The pressure groups who urge special treatment for gifted children, and who are most vociferous in their criticism of schools, both primary and secondary, for their neglect or mishandling of this kind of child, are often thinking of children with exceptionally high measured IQ, who nevertheless fail to flourish at school. Such children are often disruptive and hard to accommodate in an ordinary class. They may be emotionally backward and babyish, they may exhibit all kinds of behaviour problems, they may find it very difficult to get on with their contemporaries. They are, in some sense of the word, 'maladjusted', in that they certainly do not adjust to ordinary school life. They are called 'gifted' simply on the basis of their high IQ scores, but they show no particular aptitude for any school subject; indeed they often do conspicuously badly in all subjects. They are simply thought to be potentially very clever, and therefore to be wasting their talents at school, while being totally lacking in motivation to employ whatever these talents are.

Secondly, and distinct from the children just described, there is a class of children who display very marked talents in certain particular fields from a very early age. The most obvious examples are those who are specially talented in mathematics and those who are specially talented in music. These children are perhaps the most properly to be referred to as the 'gifted', for their gifts are obvious and outstanding. They probably number about two per cent of the whole school population at any given time.

Last, there are children who are simply very clever, and often very industrious, very ambitious and very highly motivated as well. These are the manifest high-fliers, who should be able to go to the university of their choice and read there whatever subject they like, and who will almost certainly emerge with a first class degree at the end. Such children may well also be very competent, even outstanding, as musicians, artists, actors, dancers and games-players. For a clever child, in this sense, will lap up whatever he is taught, will exercise his imagination in whatever subject he is introduced to, will have the necessary powers of concentration to practise his skills, and, unless he is in some way physically disabled, will probably have good coordination along with his other gifts.

In the days of the grammar school, the third group I have mentioned did not constitute a problem. They were the natural scholarship-winners, the top of the eleven-plus list, the success children. Good grammar schools flourished from a steady supply of such children, whom they loved and encouraged, and of whom they were proud. But other less talented children greatly benefited from having them in the same class, and from associating with them in all sorts of ways. They differ from the first group of children by the fact that their IQ may not be as high (though of course it may be); but, more importantly, by the fact that they tend actually to succeed, their characters, their powers of concentration, their adaptability making them natural winners, just as members of the first group may seem natural wasters, failers and losers. They differ from the second group in that their talents are more general, less intensely specialized, than those of the specifically 'gifted'.

Such a tripartite classification is obviously deceptively neat. There will be overlaps among the three classes, and there will be talented children who do not fit exactly into any of the three. Nevertheless, as a broad classification it will do; and if the categories are recognizable, then that in itself is a sufficient explanation of the difficulty of finding a single solution to the problem of how such children should be treated within the comprehensive system.

But there is another, more depressing reason for the difficulty of providing for gifted children, and that is the attitude of teachers to the educational needs of those children who, actually or potentially, come at the top of the continuum of ability. There is an extreme reluctance to admit that children who are clever have special educational needs.

The general view is that they can look after themselves. They can pick things up easily, so they don't really need teaching. And if they do sometimes seem to be sacrificed to the majority, this is inevitable, and probably only fair. The connection between academic success and economic prosperity, that very connection which rendered the eleven-plus examination suspect, and lay behind the educational thinking of the 1950s and 1960s, operates to the disadvantage of the clever child. Not only is he thought to be clever enough to look after himself educationally, but he is supposed to have middle-class advantages as well. Too often his middle-class, professional parents are thought to be pushing him ahead in an over-ambitious and competitive way. The élite and the intellectual, the talented and the privileged are all disastrously jumbled together, and many teachers want to have nothing to do with any of them. So much emerged clearly from the DES investigation of the teaching of the gifted, published in 1977.

So what is to be done? Denying that there are such children in any particular school, or maintaining that, if there are, they must swim along as best they can with the majority (the responses most frequently made by teachers to questions about these children) is not enough. There is increasing evidence that these children are badly catered for in many of our schools. And a failure to cater for their needs is a failure which society can ill afford, quite apart from the frustration and misery which may result for individual children.

The first of our categories of children undoubtedly need to be treated cautiously, tenderly and with the minimum of dogmatism. Anything is worth trying with them, as with other maladjusted children, which may enable them to begin to learn and to enjoy working. Once they enjoy it, there is hope that they may begin to use their high intelligence to some effect. But since we are largely ignorant of the causes of their problems, we cannot be over-confident in our interventions to remove the effects. It is almost certain that such children will need to be taught for at least part of every day either by themselves or at least in very small groups. Ordinary rewards and punishments will probably be ineffective with them, since they do not value the things that ordinary children value, and will be, for example, largely unmoved by the kinds of deprivations which might be punishment to other children, or the kinds of inducements which might act as spurs or rewards.

Some sort of breakthrough may come if one subject can be found which really grips the child's imagination and in which, probably for some purely internal motive, he wants to do well. This discovery may come through the influence of one particular teacher, or for no discernible reason at all. Whatever the details of the method employed, such children must be treated as having their own special problems of adjustment, and only if these can be solved can they begin to do as well as they should. But it may be a very slow process, and frustrating for teachers and parents alike. The fact that such a difficult child has a high IQ and may show flashes of brilliance makes it all the more unbearable. When he totally fails to concentrate, when he does anything rather than work, it is almost inevitable that people should reproach him: 'it isn't as if you were *stupid*'. Whether a comprehensive school will be able to educate such children as these will entirely depend upon whether there is an efficient system of withdrawal from ordinary classes into small groups, or even a system which allows individual tuition. It will also depend on the imagination of the teachers, and their willingness to try things that may actually interest the particular child.

It may be necessary for such a child, at least temporarily, to go to a special school, where there may be the possibility of individual teaching, and where the preparedness of the teachers for difficult, destructive and awkward behaviour will be greater. But such a measure ought to be regarded as short-term. And even if such a child is educated at a special school, it is of the greatest importance that he should not be allowed to neglect the ordinary educational requirements demanded of all intelligent children. He must be given every possible encouragement to sit for public examinations, and to adopt for himself the goals of university and career which his contemporaries will have before them. If there is too much emphasis on understanding, care and therapy he may miss his education altogether. To recognize that a child is maladjusted is to recognize that he needs preliminary help, or perhaps help on the side, to adjust to an ordinary educational programme. But as soon as he can profit from it, and perhaps before he can profit from it fully, he needs to be taught, and to be led or pushed along the regular educational road. To overlook this is to deprive him of what he most urgently needs. Education, actually learning to understand things or to do them properly, is by far the best form of therapy. The needs of this group of 'gifted' children are largely, though not exclusively, educational needs.

The second category of children, the manifestly gifted, for whom perhaps the term should be reserved, present far less difficult problems. At least they are enthusiastic about their speciality, they want to work at it, they are capable of extra-ordinary feats of concentration, and they are, in general, such as their parents and their schools may be proud of. But although in these ways they are easier, their problems are by no means always satisfactorily dealt with at present.

It has long been a part of Labour educational policy, and doubtless of Conservative too, that a child who exhibits great talent in music or dancing may need to attend a special school, where enough time can be devoted both to expert teaching and to practice. Such children are allowed to have special educational needs, sometimes for boarding education. Moreover a number of special musically-orientated schools have come into existence under various local authorities.

There is some merit in this policy. At least it shows that a small class of gifted children has been recognized to exist, and their special educational needs have been acknowledged. But it is by no means certain that special schools are the best solution. There is just as strong an argument for the integration of the specially talented into ordinary schools as there is for the integration of the handicapped. For if the special needs of the one can be met in ordinary schools by a system of special programmes, of withdrawal from normal classes and of extra help where it is needed, then so can the needs of the other. Moreover, just as the concept of the handicapped should be extended so that anyone who has fallen behind in any way at school should be able to benefit from special teaching, so the concept of the gifted should certainly be extended beyond the talented dancers and musicians.

But let us consider these musicians first, since they are perhaps the most familiar example. It is undoubtedly the case that musical talent makes itself known very early, if there is anyone interested in noticing such things. Schools are getting better at testing children's musical potential at an early stage, and many local authorities are extremely enterprising in the arrangements for instrumental lessons for primary and secondary school children. In any case, since musical talents tend to be inherited, and also fostered by a musical environment, most of the really outstanding child musicians are the children of musicians, and are seen to be talented by their parents. Detection of talent, then, is not the great problem.

The difficulty is that musicians, especially string players, need to start to learn their instruments at a very early age; they need to be really well taught and they need to have time every day to practise, ideally under supervision, while they are small. Moreover, for a potential professional it is a tremendous disadvantage not to be expert on the piano as well as his other instrument, so the child will need two instrumental lessons each week and time for two lots of practising. It seems a formidable programme, especially for a child of eight or nine.

All the same, it can be managed very well; but only if the school, the local authority and the parents act in partnership. If such a partnership can be set up, if the parents can be truly involved in the progress of the child, to the extent of attending some of his lessons, and learning enough to supervise the practising at home; if the school can be brought to realize that this child is a special child, who will sometimes miss other school activities for the sake of music; if the local authority is prepared to ensure that good teaching is available, then, in principle there need be no difficulties which cannot be overcome.

As the child grows up, the need for flexibility and understanding on the part of the school increases. It is essential that everyone in the school should take music seriously, in the sense that a music lesson will be a permissible reason for not attending some other school lesson; that subjects may be dropped for the sake of more practising time, and this should be taken as a matter of course. In this kind of atmosphere, even if the child has to miss whole days of school in order to travel to a lesson, then there is no reason why even the most high-powered musical child should not flourish at an ordinary school.

Of course such things are easier for a child in a large town. There is more likely to be adequate teaching within reach, for one thing. It may be that, in a few cases, the only way that a child can get the education he needs will be to move to another school. But even in this case it is far better if he can move to an ordinary school which happens to be better placed geographically, or to have a greater concern for music, than to a designated music special school. For in the ordinary school, the child will have the benefit of ordinary teaching in his non-musical subjects. He may take *fewer* subjects than his peers, but they will all be taught in the same way, and in the same classes. If he decides that, after all, he does not want to pursue a career in music, it will be easier and less traumatic for him to change course; and the school will be in general better equipped to ensure that he keeps his options open by taking the minimum necessary academic subjects. The same kind of arguments apply to dancing, at least in the early years of a child's education, though the problems of adequate teaching and practising may be rather more intractable.

A further great merit of educating these gifted children in ordinary schools is that the very same principles of flexibility and variety may be applied to children who exhibit talent in other directions. Mathematicians also reveal their abilities early, and there is no doubt at all that when a child is a naturally gifted mathematician he needs special teaching, and the opportunity to go ahead into his subject as fast and as far as he wants.

There should, in every comprehensive school, be at least one member of the staff who, while not a mathematical genius himself, can recognize genius when he sees it, and can give the child work which will excite and challenge him, and allow him to exercise his imagination in his own way. It is useless to think that such a child can be taught with his contemporaries in class. If the mathematics teaching in the school is good, and if the children are properly divided into sets, then it may be that for part of the time the talented child can work with the top set. But he will, all the same, need more than they have, and it must be allowable for him to withdraw from some classes, in order to follow his bent. In some schools where there is a child of great mathematical gifts there are arrangements for him to be taught by someone outside school, from a university or polytechnic, and this seems to be an exciting and imaginative plan. Once again everything turns on the school's readiness to adapt the normal curriculum to the educational needs of the individual child, and to recognize that in this case he will probably have more insight into his own needs and his own capacities than any of his teachers has.

There are probably no other talents so obvious as those in music, dancing and mathematics. At least where there are other outstanding talents, they are more likely to be fairly easily accommodated within the ordinary school curriculum. For example, a child who exhibits particular gifts in art will simply work better than his contemporaries, and will probably be encouraged to go on with his work, but will not be held up by the fact that other children cannot do as well as he. Similarly, if a child is a gifted writer, or shows a peculiar ability for historical understanding, he will not need to be withdrawn from the ordinary classes in order to exercise his talent. He will simply write better what he has to write. As for linguistic talents, it has already been said that every child who possibly can should start a foreign language in the first year of secondary school, and that children should be divided into sets for their language teaching as soon as possible. If there is a child who displays marked talent and interest, then he should be encouraged to start another foreign language in the second year, and he should be permitted to give up some other subject if necessary in order to do this. The principle of flexibility and variety must operate here, as elsewhere.

We have now probably already reached the third category

of gifted children, the all-round bright, the generally clever child, the old-fashioned top of the grammar school intake. It is perhaps for these children that most anxiety is felt by critics of the comprehensive schools, if only because they are the most numerous of the 'gifted'. These are the children who will be good at languages but equally good at science subjects; who will be competent at mathematics and take pleasure in it, but also intelligent and perceptive about literature or history. Such children will tackle any task they are given, and will on the whole be glad to. The only difficulty they present is that they need to be given a great many tasks, and they get through them fast and efficiently. At some stage, too, they will have to be given help and advice about how to choose between subjects, any of which they would probably be competent to pursue in their higher education.

Not so very long ago it would have been assumed that most of the resources of the educational system (including, of course, the resources of higher education) would be devoted to just such children as these. Now they are in danger of being starved of resources, as the social desirability of educating the less well-endowed, and the actual psychological possibility of educating children with sensory or mental handicaps, are more and more appreciated. It is essential to redress the balance. At present there is a tendency among teachers and educationalists to underestimate the needs of the clever child, indeed almost to resent him, and certainly to resent those parents who seem to be demanding something extra for their children, on the grounds that they are clever. If this resentment is to be eliminated, then the habit (already referred to) of identifying the academically successful with the élite, the privileged with the clever, must be broken. (It would be better still if the élite and privileged were not resented either, but to effect such a change is unnecessary for the purely educational goal here in view.)

The identification has taken root largely because of the growing tendency among educationalists as well as others to think in sociological terms, rather than in terms of individuals. It has always been true that the middle classes contained the largest number of academically successful children. Yet up to the Second World War, and even for a time thereafter, it was still perfectly possible to encourage working-class children to compete with their middle-class contemporaries for academic success, through scholarships, and later the eleven-plus entry to grammar school. Of course it was very likely that such children would turn into members of the middle class somewhere along the line. As we have seen already, the whole concept of equality of opportunity in education was based on the assumption that we had a competitive system and that some individual children from the working classes would make it to the top.

But since educational competition, and the consequential notion of training children up to succeed in it, is an essentially middle-class concept (or so it is alleged) then it was this which had to be abandoned in the interests of the classless society. Schools ought not to aim at academic success, this argument runs, for even if individual working-class children can attain it, it will always be a middle-class aim. Schools, it is said, must aim at a different kind of goal altogether, and one which is acceptable not to individual and exceptional members of the working class, but to the working class as a whole.

It is against this background that the comparative neglect of the clever child in school has grown up. But we cannot, by thinking like sociologists, deny the actual purpose of educating people, whether at school or at university, which is to enable them to live the best lives they are individually capable of, after education is finished. And there is no doubt that for many of them this best kind of life will be a life of intellectual, if not academic, enterprise, for which they need the skills and the knowledge that school and university will give them. In society as it is, a university degree is necessary for those entering a whole range of professions, and it is at least a desirable preliminary to many more. As long as this is so, and as long as entry to the universities is competitive, then it is right that schools should teach what the universities want taught.

It is irrelevant (even if it is intelligible) to say that the universities represent middle-class values. Even if this were so, it would still be a deprivation if those who wanted to go to university were unable to do so because they had not been properly taught at school. Schools must be to some extent conservative. They must, that is, teach children *what it is already demanded that they should know*. It is inappropriate to go very far in schools with experiments in new forms of knowledge, as long as there are pupils in the schools who actually need the old forms.

But the kind of teaching they need demands a commitment to a certain amount of accuracy, detail and precision, as well as to the more exciting kinds of creative or imaginative thinking. It is of no use to children, for example, to have the general concept of different languages. They may need to know the grammar and syntax of one or two particular languages if they are to go on with their language studies after school. A broad view of the interconnections between different sciences will not do for the potential doctor or physicist, though if he has this as well, so much the better. In every subject, the child who may want to go on with it after school will have to be taught in some detail, and by someone who is himself an expert in the subject. Without teaching, it is impossible that he should learn what he needs to know.

At some stage, then, the clever and ambitious children in any given subject, must be separated from the less clever or less ambitious, and simply be taught *more* than the latter need or want to know. And at least in the case of languages and mathematics, this separation is likely to have to take place as early as the first year in secondary school.

It is to protect the rights of the gifted, in the third sense of that term, that limits have to be placed upon mixed-ability teaching, and setting has to be instituted as a normal part of school life. But if this is to be done, then teachers must believe in it, and must actually come to believe that it is the only way in which the aims of education can be achieved. Once again, there is no reason in principle why a comprehensive ideal cannot embrace the ideal of educating the gifted, as well as every other child; indeed if 'comprehensive' means anything, this should be part of the aim.

5

Examinations

Throughout the preceding chapters, mention has been made from time to time of tests and examinations at different stages of a child's educational career. This chapter will sum up a policy on examinations which would serve the interests of all children at school.

First, it is necessary to say something in defence of the notion of examinations in general, since for fifteen or twenty years it has been suspect; and even if it is now coming back into favour, it still needs to be supported by argument, if it is not to be dismissed as reactionary, black-paper stuff. The arguments against examinations are familiar enough. It is said that they inhibit and terrify pupils, that they prevent teachers from innovating and experimenting with the curriculum, and, above all, that they are divisive. In any comprehensive school there will necessarily be those who cannot take examinations at all, and those who, if they do, will fail, as well as those who succeed. So either, it is argued, a new kind of examination should be devised which it is impossible to fail, or there should be no examinations at all.

Enough has been said already about the need for 'setting' in schools, and the disadvantages of too much mixed-ability teaching to suggest that 'divisiveness', though the word is derogatory, is not something which should be eliminated from schools. It is an essential part of proper education that children should be taught as far as possible according to their needs.

The fact is that it is perfectly possible for children to accept that they are more (or less) successful than some of their contemporaries in various school subjects (just as they have no difficulty in accepting it in the case of sports and athletics). Children of different abilities can be friendly, and neither resentful nor envious of success. If such mutual acceptance is not possible in any particular school, then this is a black mark against the school. One of the moral lessons a school, and indeed a family, should teach is that other people are worthy of respect and affection even if, in competition with oneself, they always win, or always lose. If this is sometimes a hard lesson to learn, that is no reason for trying to eliminate competition from schools which are, of all places, the best fitted to teach such lessons.

But, it is argued, a child who fails in examinations is 'labelled' a failure and this will affect him for the rest of his life. I believe that there is a great deal of absurd prejudice summed up in the fashionable horror of 'labelling'. There is, of course, some truth in the view that it is damaging to give a dog a bad, or for that matter a good, name. People may try hard to live up to the rôle they are expected to play. Everyone who has ever been in a school staff room knows that there are some children who provoke a groan every time their names are mentioned, and at whose door the sins of a whole class are perpetually laid. But this is really not at all peculiar to schools, and it certainly has little or nothing to do with the examination system. Teachers certainly have a duty not to allow a child to get stuck with a reputation which he may never have deserved, or which he may long have outgrown. But there will be a danger of such reputations being acquired whether or not there are tests and examinations; and they are acquired just as readily outside as inside school. That there is a perfectly general duty on us all to be fair and charitable in our dealings with one another cannot possibly constitute an argument against a system of examinations.

The arguments against examinations then are not very serious. There are, on the other hand, many positive arguments in favour of them. First, they act as an incentive, a stimulus to both teachers and pupils to work in an orderly way towards a common goal. It is a strong bond between teacher and pupil to have a common enemy, the external examiner, far stronger, often, than any more self-conscious effort a teacher may make to show that he is on the side of the 'kids'. If this is thought to be a disreputable motive, whether for teamwork or for work of any kind, it can only be said that it is effective. Nor is it effective, as it is sometimes alleged, only for the clever and successful child. On the contrary, one of the difficulties of teaching the less able child at present is there is no satisfactory incentive for him. Examinations, then, must be taken by as many children as possible; in some form or other by at least eighty, perhaps ninety per cent of all children in school.

Secondly local authorities, who have to allocate educational resources, need the results of common, standardized examinations in order to discover where resources of different kinds are most needed. It is often suggested that in order to produce this kind of information it is not necessary to examine the individual pupils at school, but only to monitor the performance of schools or classes within schools as a whole. The concept of monitoring is not altogether clear; but too often it entails simply discovering how a system works, rather than trying to find out in detail whether it works well or ill for the individual pupil. Assessing the performance of children by means of various internal tests should indeed have a place in schools, but it is not enough.

Assessment of this kind is intended, to quote the Schools Council (Working Paper 53), to provide teachers with a 'reasonably accurate indication of how their pupils' basic skills compare with those in other classes or schools'. With the help of such tests, teachers can correct weaknesses in a whole group, before they become too marked. Now this kind of thing is good; it is a formalized extension of what teachers tend to do anyway, that is to compare the performance of one whole class with, let us say, the same class last year, or in the school he taught at before. But the paper already quoted goes on to insist that such assessment should be mainly *descriptive*. It should simply reveal where a class as a whole has got to and how they perform. It does not, says the paper firmly, test 'achievement', for no one can fail to achieve. *What* they achieve will simply be noted in a non-evaluative way. Such is the intention. There is nothing wrong with such tests, but they are no substitute for examinations, for in fact the individual pupils are not, in taking such purely descriptive tests, being asked to do the same sort of thing: they are not being asked to *try*.

Thirdly, there needs to be a dependable national standard of comparable individual achievement which employers, colleges of further and higher education and universities can use and readily understand. Common external examinations are the only means which can achieve this end.

Finally, teachers who are reluctant to allow their pupils to be examined, however high their motives, are actually depriving their pupils of an experience which, though it can be alarming, is valuable in itself. Obviously one must ensure that children do not sit for examinations where they have no hope of being able to do anything at all. But, given a suitable examination, a child's confidence may be enormously improved by the proof that he is able to do *something* entirely on his own. There are many experiences in real life where the sudden thought strikes one 'I am on my own now. No one can do this for me. It is up to me'. The examination is one of the first of such experiences. To come to an examination, however simple, well-prepared and able to fend for oneself is a triumph, and one which is in itself educationally valuable. Teachers should not assume that their pupils are incapable of so much resolution and independence.

How, then, should examinations in secondary schools be structured? There are many possible solutions to this problem. I shall outline one which seems to be both consistent and useful to the children themselves.

In primary school, there should be no examinations, but the common curriculum outlined in chapter 2 should be followed, and should indeed occupy most of the school timetable. Then, when children have had time to accustom themselves a little to their new school, and get to know their class and their class teacher, they should have some standardized tests, perhaps prepared within each local authority, or perhaps available nationally, in the subjects from the common curriculum which are to be deemed examinable; at this stage this means reading and comprehension, writing, mathematics and perhaps practical science. These tests, however they are prepared, should be marked by teachers within the school, and should be used as the basis for 'setting', which is crucial to the success of much in the comprehensive school. Obviously this setting would be provisional in the first term; but there will probably not be a very large number of changes. The setting for modern languages will have to be finalized later, since the vast majority of children will be starting the first foreign language for the first time on reaching secondary school. But it will be on the basis of the first test that some children will be selected ·for extra work in English instead of a foreign language of any kind. (It must be remembered that many of the children who need this extra help will be children for whom in fact English is not their first language, or not the language they speak at home. For them it is essential that they are taught to read, write and speak fluent English, so that they do not fall further behind.) These first tests, while standardized, will not in any full sense be public examinations, but parents should automatically be informed of how their children have emerged from the tests.

At the end of the first two years will come the first properly public examination, set, it is to be hoped, by a regional examination board. There is everything to be said for having eight or ten such boards, rather than a central examining body. For one thing, schools get to know and trust their own examining boards. For another thing if, as is to be expected, teachers have an increasing part to play as members of the examining boards, more teachers can be involved if there is a diversity of boards, and it will be easier for them to attend meetings in their own region.

I do not believe that any system will long command the confidence and respect of employers or universities in which teachers set papers and mark them specifically for their own pupils (as in the present Mode 3 of the O level examinations). But I do believe that teachers have an enormously important part to play in the setting and marking of papers which are taken by all or most of the schools in a particular region. These newly constituted boards, then, consisting partly of teachers, should set and mark the first public examination, which might be called 'Basic level' or 'B level'.

I do not think that there should be any age specification as far as this (or any other) examination is concerned. The only rule should be that it may not be taken in the primary school, however ready a child may be to take it. It should be an examination literally common to all children, should *normally* be taken at the end of the second year of secondary school, should be a pass/fail examination, in four sections (literacy, numeracy, scientific competence and a modern language) and should all, or in parts, be able to be taken again and again until it is passed.

It may be objected that such a common test must be valueless, because if it is to be attempted by *all* children at school (all, that is, except those with very severe learning difficulties) it will inevitably be far too easy for the top fifty per cent of children. But this is no objection. If it is a test of a minimum necessary standard then of course it is to be expected that a majority of children will find it easy. But that only means that they will take the test in their stride, without much specific teaching for it, just as many children used to take the eleven-plus without even noticing that that was what they were doing. The better the foundation in the basic subject at primary school, and the first year at secondary school, the easier the test will be for an ever increasing number of children, many of whom, indeed, may be allowed to take the test before the end of the third year, if that is convenient. Those who have taken and passed their B levels can begin to choose extra subjects, even to drop some subjects with a view to their O levels, which they will take at the end of their fifth year at school.

O levels will be intended for all those children who now take either CSE or O level. Children who have great difficulty with their B levels can continue to work for them while also working for a number of O level subjects. O levels should be a single subject examination, that is one could take one or many subjects in the same term, one could take an extra subject at any time, whether in school or outside, and there should be no intrinsic demand for any particular balance of subjects within the examination. As I have argued already, any demand for balance among the O level subjects should not come from the examination system itself, but from universities or employers in the outside world.

If there is to be a successful single system of examination, it must be very flexible. The studies so far undertaken to see whether a single system would work have been very unsatisfactory, because in many cases there was a desire among those conducting the studies to show that one syllabus could do for all children. This is both unnecessary and impossible. It must be recognized that within the same examination there can be different syllabuses in, let us say, English literature, history and mathematics, and indeed different methods of examination. There should be many different routes to the attainment of an O level certificate. It should be possible for some children to work at long-term projects, externally examined; for others to go outside school into work experience, about which they could write or answer questions as part of the examination. Some subjects should be purely practical, others purely academic. There should be full examinations in spoken modern languages, separate from the written examinations. (Of course children could take both.) In general it should be possible for some children to take all academic subjects, others to take all practical subjects, others to take a mixture. The balance, if it existed, would be such as was demanded by the universities and employers.

In the final two years at school those who stayed on would be working for A levels, which, it is hoped, might be divided into major and minor subjects. Sixth formers would normally take two major and three minor subjects, or three major and two minor. Minor subjects would fall, in standard, between O and A level. It would be perfectly acceptable for some sixth formers to take more O levels and some minor A levels. Thus almost everyone who left school, whether at sixteen or at eighteen, would leave with some sort of a certificate to mark the work successfully achieved at school. In the bottom twenty per cent of the ability range there would be those who would leave, even at eighteen (and it is to be hoped that many could stay on so long) with a certificate of B levels only. Most children would leave at sixteen with a certificate at B level, but, in addition, with one marking O level passes in various subjects. Those who left at eighteen would have a B level certificate, and their second certificate would have passes at O level, major A level and

minor A level, in various combinations. Such a system would
be intelligible to the outside world, and usable as a
qualification for the next stage of education.

   It is often said that if a child is allowed to give up his B
level subjects at fourteen he will forget them: he will forget
how to calculate or how to speak his somewhat rudimentary
French. This may well be true. But I believe that the evils of
compulsion at adolescence may be worse. If there are to be
compulsory subjects after this, I think that the pressure to
take them must come from outside school. The more
professions make O level passes compulsory in a modern
language, a science and a mathematical subject as well as
some 'literary' subject (not necessarily English literature, but
any subject which involves the writing of continuous prose)
the better the general spread of subjects in a school will
become; and it will be possible seriously to advise pupils that
they will be losing valuable chances if they do not cover a
reasonable range. But if, in spite of this, there are children
who obstinately refuse to work at anything which is not a
science or, let us say, a craft subject, then it seems to me it is
better that they should work at that than at nothing. After
all, it is always possible to collect the necessary O levels later,
after school.

   A system of examination such as is here suggested is highly
flexible and various. The eight or ten proposed boards would
obviously develop, as the examining boards do now, their
own characteristics. In order to ensure that the system in
general had the necessary credibility, it would be absolutely
essential to have a single validating body to ensure com-
parability of results between one region and another. This
would be a proper function of the Schools Council. Indeed it
had exactly these powers until 1970, and should assume them
again without delay. If this were done, and if the examinations were structured in the way just outlined, there would
be a consistent and workable system that would accommodate a very large majority of all children at school. There
would be no school which could say 'we do not do O level' or
'we do not do B level' (though if there were schools without
sixth forms they would not do A level). There would be a uniformity, to this extent, between all schools, public and private.

But of course, to make the system work, once again it is absolutely essential for teachers to be ready to separate children according to the syllabus they are to follow, and to the papers in the O-level examination they are to sit. Neither pleas of lack of resources nor doctrinaire refusals to admit that some children are more academic or simply cleverer than others should be accepted as an excuse for failing to take these decisions.

If a school genuinely has not the teachers or the space to allow setting, then the children who need a course they cannot get should be moved to another school, or even allowed to take all their O-level examination subjects at a college of further education, alongside grown-ups. Parents must be persuaded that teachers actually want their children to succeed. Somehow the theory that all examinations are competitive and that competition is wicked must be undermined. Only so can children have their educational needs fulfilled, and parents have their fears of comprehensive education allayed.

6

Moral Education

So far, the argument has been concerned with the best form of academic and practical education. I have tried to outline a curriculum flexible and adaptable enough for the most and the least able pupils, one which will have as its firm aim the maximization of both the competence and the happiness of those who follow it.

But there is another aspect of life at school equally important to society and to the children themselves as members of society, and that is moral education.

Of no other aspect of education have greater demands been made; no other aspect has attracted so much discussion and strident criticism. It is a confused and complicated issue.

On the one hand, there is fear of indoctrination, of extreme pressure on children, of arbitrary rules and equally capricious punishments. On the other hand there is a fear of total moral indifference, either because it seems impossible to interest children in morality, or because in principle it is held wrong to do so, in a world where all moralities are relative, no standards absolute.

There is no doubt, however, that parents hope that their children will learn to behave well, that they will learn to distinguish right from wrong at school; and they are right to assume that this must be part of education. For children spend a great part of their waking life at school, which is the kind of institution in which moral questions necessarily come up, for practical decision. It would be absurd, therefore, if the school had absolutely no moral lessons to teach. For children are not morally competent, let alone morally good, by nature.

Moral education must, therefore, be undertaken by any

school. But what form such education ought to take is far from clear, despite all the books written about it. The first point to establish is that moral education is to be distinguished from religious education. As I argued in the introductory chapter, religious education should be an element in every school curriculum, whether it remains legally compulsory or not. An understanding of what religion is like, what it has actually effected in the world, what it has inspired people to do and to create, what actual beliefs have been held, all this is something which no education should omit. And of course if a teacher or a pupil is personally religious, it is certain that his notion of morality will be actually connected with his religion, his moral standards drawn from the teachings of the church.

But a knowledge of religion, even an understanding of it, is not the same as religion itself, and it is the *knowledge and understanding* which the school should set out to teach. Such knowledge may greatly excite and interest pupils who are not themselves at all religious. Indeed the time is ripe for a renaissance of religious education. Ignorance of even the most elementary facts about, for example, the Christian year, or the best worn Bible stories is widespread, as anyone engaged in the teaching of literature would testify. It is no longer possible for a teacher to assume that most of the members of a class will at least officially belong to some church or other. It is also no longer possible to assume a wide-spread acceptance of religion. On the contrary, the whole concept of religion is totally unknown to a vast number of children at school. Therefore religion can be presented as something strange, something which may add a new dimension to ordinary life, and something which has in the past inspired saints, artists, writers and musicians, and may continue to do so in the future. The modern trend in theology, much as it may be deplored in some church cirlces, of treating Christianity as myth, and the recognition nonetheless that myth may convey the truth, makes the teaching of religion far easier and far more rewarding than when a teacher was bound at least to appear to find an answer to every factual doubt a child might raise. The teaching of religion need no longer be dogmatic in order to be genuine.

But to introduce children to this extra dimension of thought and feeling is not necessarily or primarily to introduce them to morality; moreover, the religious education offered by a school should not attempt to *make* anyone either religious or indeed irreligious. On the other hand, the moral education offered should attempt to make the pupils morally good. The two must therefore be distinct, whatever the connections may seem to be, for those who are actually themselves committed to religion.

But having made this purely negative point, it remains to try to establish what moral education is, if it is not the same as religious education. Is there, for example, to be a lesson on the timetable called 'morality' or ME? A number of educationalists have argued that there should be. The content of these lessons should be, they say, to teach children how to conduct moral arguments, and how to base their moral convictions on good reasons. The lessons would be a species of philosophy lessons, partly concerned to distinguish argument from blind prejudice, partly to practise the art of uncovering presuppositions and presumptions, and submitting these to rational scrutiny. Examples could be taken and examined, different rôles could be played, in order to make the exemplary situations come alive. Independence of thought and ingenuity of argument should be encouraged.

I can see the interest, even the value, of some such lessons, at least for relatively senior members of a school. I think there is everything to be said for a lesson perhaps specifically connected with 'current affairs' or 'civics' in which key moral issues which arise in the real world are discussed. Examples of such issues could be drawn from industry (how morally wrong do we really believe it to be to use 'slush funds', for example, or how ought picketing to be conducted) from politics (how strong is the actual obligation of politicians to refrain from deceiving the public?) or from the general areas of social life (the legalization of cannabis, the control of the sale of alcohol, the morality of advertisements). Such discussions are useful and highly educational, and with a good, intelligent teacher, or a good television programme, can be adapted for pupils of high or of low ability. They form an essential part of the general education of children in the realities of the contemporary world.

But it is extremely doubtful whether such lessons as these, good and necessary as they are, have any very marked effect on the actual conduct of children, whether in school or outside it. Being clear-headed about, let us say, the ill effects of the portrayal of violence on television, or the sale of pornographic literature, or of tax evasion will not on the whole make a difference to whether a member of the school is himself cruel or kind, honest or dishonest, forgiving or vindictive. A man (or a child) may be knowledgeable, rational, logical and astute, yet not morally good.

For to be morally good is to have a certain sort of character, not a certain sort of ability, nor a certain sort of knowledge, and so the question is whether anything can be done at school to help a child to develop this kind of character. Or, in well-worn terms, 'can virtue be taught?' If it cannot be taught, if a school can do nothing towards the development of a good character, then the belief that schools should teach morality must be abandoned, for it will lead to demands which are impossible to satisfy.

Perhaps, before pursuing the question directly, some very general observations may be in place. It is peculiarly difficult to discuss questions of morals dispassionately and in such a way as to carry conviction, partly because of radically changing fashions in the common moral vocabulary. Perhaps 'fashion' is an unduly pejorative word. There are good reasons why certain concepts become unacceptable in this semi-philosophical field. But examples will bring out the facts, however they are to be described. No one who spoke of 'duty' in general (as opposed to particular 'duties') would now be likely to gain much of a hearing; and similarly the notion of 'character-forming', much in use in school prospectuses in the early part of the century, is now a matter for jokes only. While moral philosophers are interested in rules, conventions, principles and commands, they are not very much concerned, on the whole, with virtues and vices. All the same, if you asked most parents what they wanted for their children, they would be more likely to answer in terms of the child's *becoming a certain sort of person* than in terms of his learning and obeying a certain set of rules by which his behaviour should be governed. All of us value highly people who both do things which we admire and do them from a certain inner motivation, a spontaneity which is different from the austere obedience to rules: they do the things, as Aristotle says, liking to do them or gladly. To be nice or nasty, lovable or detestable is to have a certain sort of character.

If we think of a man as having a likeable or admirable character, then we can predict, not, it is true, exactly what he will do, but that whatever he does will be all right, may even be better than anything we could have predicted. If, for example, he is a generous man, then we know that what he does will be motivated by generosity, and even if it does not at first sight look like a generous act, it will turn out in the end to have been one. For to have a certain character is to be trustworthy in a certain respect. And this is what most parents would like their children to be.

Of course to have a good and reliable character and to obey rules are not incompatible. There is the kind of character which essentially makes and adheres to rules in all the circumstances of life. But this is only *one* kind of good character, and not perhaps the most desirable. Most people would prefer a child (or a friend) who was naturally and spontaneously honest, loyal, truthful and capable of gratitude than one who displayed such virtues because it was laid down in a code of rules, which he believed he had to obey. Moreover rules tend to lay down how one should behave in well specified situations; a good character, on the other hand, is one we can trust even if circumstances are new and strange. Thus if a child seems reliable, kind, generous and truthful at school, and this is in his nature, we feel confident that in the unknown world beyond school he will, in all probability, be equally admirable in his behaviour. To be of good character is to be such as to be able to adapt to new situations in a more or less predictably good way. Thus, if at school there were a way of developing in children good character, however unappealing such an aim may sound, this would be to look ahead to the rest of life. It would conform to the general aims of education upon which we have so frequently insisted. It is not so much what happens at school that matters, but what happens afterwards.

There are, however, those who believe that all that a school can properly teach, in the matter of morals, is certain rules, with the reasons why they are imposed. It is necessary therefore to digress briefly on the subject of rules at school. In the first place, it will be obvious that what is under discussion are not 'school rules'. as normally understood. These rules are generally only remotely connected with morality. They are rules of convenience or of safety, entirely necessary for any institution, especially an institution containing children, but not particularly leading to morally good conduct, if obeyed, nor morally bad, if disobeyed. They regulate such things as obtaining permission for absence, the payment of fees (where appropriate), the wearing of uniform, the marking of clothes, the hours of attendance, and perhaps they mark out certain geographical areas of the school which are not permitted for general use.

It is extremely important that such regulations should not be confused with moral rules. If children are rebuked or even punished for breaking the school rules it must be made absolutely clear that it is not a moral offence which has been committed. Nothing is more confusing to a child, nor ultimately more damaging to morality, than to speak as though the breach of regulations about length of hair or kinds of permitted footwear were a moral offence. Nothing, alas, is more typical of a bad school than this kind of confusion. It may be proper to punish people for a breach of school rules; but if so it must be made clear that this is in the nature of a fine or penalty, not a punishment for a moral wrong.

But what of specifically moral rules? Ought a school to draw up a code of morality and teach this? There are many theorists who believe that it is this and only this which a school is entitled to do, and that, for every rule taught, a reason should be given. I dissent from this view. For I believe that morality is not a matter of reason, nor therefore of *reasons for* the existence of certain rules. Such reasons are likely to turn on the consequences of observing the code or breaking it, and on calculation of what will or might happen if the code were generally to be broken, by people as a whole. Such calculations will not, I believe, by themselves influence people's behaviour. On the contrary, morality is essentially, and not just by chance, a matter of experiencing certain common, shared sentiments. No code will be seriously embraced unless a child believes in the rules, feels that they are right, and is motivated to obedience to them by the feeling that he would be ashamed to break them. To give reasons for the rules is not enough to generate a motive to obey.

How then are such feelings to be introduced? To argue that special morals lessons on the timetable, or lists of rules pinned up on the walls will prove ineffective is not to say that there can be no teaching of morality at all. It is here perhaps that the 'hidden curriculum'—what the school teaches apart from what appears on the timetable—becomes important. In all kinds of ways, what is expected of a child can be made known in the classroom, in the playground, about the school; in matters of courtesy, fairness, honesty, kindness, tolerance and good humour. Approval and disapproval, praise and blame, these are the methods by which the concept of morality is first introduced to a child at home. And school is in this respect no different, except that at school morality must begin to take in the interests of people in no way connected with the child, and perhaps quite different from himself.

The scope of moral behaviour widens, but the way in which a child begins to think in moral terms remains the same. Whatever the exact stages of moral thinking a child goes through, it is certain that for a long time (perhaps always) he is dependent on the opinion of his elders and of his contemporaries, first as the source, and then as the reinforcement of his own dawning consciousness of what will or will not do, in the way of behaviour. The Greek notion of *shame* as the important arbiter of morality is peculiarly appropriate at school, though also, in my view, appropriate in the world of grown up morality as well.

It must not be thought that because incidents at school may be trivial, they cannot form the subject matter of true morality. Although the actual circumstances in which a teacher behaves unfairly to a child may not be dramatic, and may seem absurd from a grownup standpoint, the child may be acutely aware of the real unfairness. If the matter over which honesty is demanded is nothing more than the possession of a pencil, or whether a child did or did not do a piece of work himself, nevertheless it is real honesty which is required and it may be just as difficult to display it, as easy to avoid it, as in more heroic circumstances. A bully in the playground is a bully nonetheless.

Teachers are often accused by parents and other grownups of making mountains out of molehills, and of living perpetually in a tiny world, where the least event is a drama. This is certainly a danger. On the other hand a child's world is, necessarily, small. And a teacher who cannot take the dramas of that world seriously is not really fit for his job. A balance has to be struck, but one thing is certain. If a teacher is not prepared to intervene in ordinary day-to-day behaviour at school, to weigh in with praise, condemnation or advice, with adjudication between conflicting claims, or the actual protection of the weak, there is no chance that he will help the characters of the children under his charge to develop in an awareness of morality.

But it is essential, if such intervention is to be effective, that the teacher himself should have moral convictions, should be felt to be firm in his beliefs, and above reproach. It is often said, and with justice, that children are quick to detect hypocrisy. They are also sharp in the exposure of weakness or vacillation. In the end, though these are harsh words, a child develops a good character largely by following a good example. This is the only way that virtue can be 'taught'.

To say this is to impose a fearful burden on the teacher. It would be far easier to confine the teaching of morality to one or two forty minute periods a week, in which moral problems could be considered away from the heat of battle, in which casuistry could take the place of action. But there is no evidence that such abstract discussion has any effect on conduct. It is one thing, as Hume says, to know virtue, another to conform the will to it. Morality is a practical matter, and in order to teach it, teachers have to practise it themselves, recognizing that what they do with conviction and consistency will in fact become a source of moral conviction in others. Parents of course carry the burden of being an example, knowingly or unknowingly, for their children. For teachers perhaps the burden is more formidable, because they should be more conscious of what they are about, and because children are more capable of judging their conduct dispassionately than the conduct of their own parents. The fact is that, whether teachers like this rôle or not, they have the responsibility of giving to a child when he is young the notion that there are good and reliable people in the world, who have strong convictions about what is right and will stick to them.

But how can teachers have strong convictions, it may be asked, if they are firmly committed to nothing except the relativity of morals? Probably no subject has been better aired in recent years, in the whole field of educational theory, than the subject of indoctrination: and no fear seems nearer the front of the minds of the teaching profession, or those who train them, than the fear of imposing on a child the values of 'society', and of failing to allow him freedom to develop his own alternative, but valid, morality. Obviously it is highly desirable that children should be taught to examine and probably to criticize the unthinking presuppositions of society as displayed for example in newspapers and the other media. But this does not mean that nothing accepted as good by society as a whole *is* good. Far from it. For how could the morality of the media be criticized, except from the standpoint of some other shared values? The notion that there are *no* shared values, no basis for a common morality, is totally misconceived, and extremely damaging.

It is true that, broadly speaking, the morality of one society or race or nation may differ from that of another; and that, within a race or nation, morals and accepted customs change from time to time. We can nearly all look back to different standards of what is acceptable behaviour, particularly in the field of sexual morality. This does not, however, entail that the only finally acceptable morality would be one which was acceptable at all times and in all places, a kind of lowest common denominator of morality. Nor does it entail, as is even more frequently supposed, that anyone who expresses moral approval or disapproval is in fact expressing only his own personal taste, but expressing it in a bogus, misleadingly authoritative form. (In fact even if morality were a matter of taste, this would be no reason for not defending it. Taste, too, changes from time to time, but any expression of taste can bring out the actual good or bad features of the object under discussion.)

For morality is something which exists within a society, and at a given time, to provide barriers, or inhibitions against certain kinds of conduct. It exists as a means for making or for critically examining actual decisions, for determining how people should behave or should not in the society he is in, in certain well-marked and broadly common areas. Man on his own, if there were such a creature, would have no need for morality. Therefore it is a pointless mistake to search for a morality independent of any society. A teacher who expresses moral views is indeed expressing the views of society, or a part of it; but this is necessarily true because he and his pupils *are* society. If he clearly apprehends what sort of behaviour now, at the time when he speaks, will make life worse for people, will cheat them, deceive them, cause unnecessary suffering, diminish their self-respect, then he is absolutely entitled to express and to share this vision, and he will inevitably state it in moral terms. For it *is* intrinsically a vision, an imaginative grasp of how things ought not (or ought) to be.

The fact is that, whatever the particular detail of morality at a given time may be, the *point* of morality as a whole remains constant, which is to mitigate and diminish the harm which people may do to one another in society. It is an attempt to ensure that people living alongside one another are better off as a whole than they would be if no moral constraints existed. To act in the consciousness of such constraints is to act morally.

Now to discuss how the constraints have been, or might be, different is to conduct an historical or philosophical or anthropological discussion, and interesting enough. But it is not practical. The teacher at school, the solicitor in his office, the doctor in his surgery, are all practical moral men. They have to act, not only to talk. Their task is to make their decisions according to their moral judgement as it is *now*.

That the teacher may also want to instruct his pupils in the historical and philosophical, the generally critical considerations surrounding morality does not excuse him from the necessity of making decisions himself, on moral grounds, and being seen so to make them.

From small beginnings, then, in school itself, the concept of morality is, if not born, at least strengthened and confirmed. So the morality of the school, of the classroom and the playground, is by far the most important feature in the moral education of a child.

The whole idea of teaching by example, of giving a child a sense of right and wrong by manifesting approval or disapproval of his behaviour depends upon there being knowledge and understanding, respect and affection between the child and the teacher. Without this, words will remain abstract, examples will be no more effective than moral stories taken from a book. Of course in any school it is to be presumed that the class teacher will know and be known by the members of his class. But this is not enough. For not all the important transactions of school life go on in the classroom; indeed as a child gets older, very little of his school life may be spent with his own specific class teacher. It is essential that there should be a fair proportion of the staff of a school who know far more children than their own class; and ideally there should be someone who knows every child. In addition, this person should know something of the parents of every child as well, especially when the children are young. Such knowledge is impossible unless the school is small.

I do not believe that the moral education of children in the sense I have defined it can possibly be carried out except in an atmosphere of mutual knowledge. And I doubt the feasibility of such knowledge in a school whose numbers run into four figures. For a small child, even for an adolescent, the impersonality of a large school is inimical to the feelings of mutual trust between pupils and teachers, and to actual shared feelings without which the teaching of morals cannot begin.

Obviously this argument for small size is too simple; and equally obviously, the older a child is, the better he will be able to overcome the disadvantages of large size. But at primary school age, no consideration ought to be allowed to outweigh the advantages of smallness. Where small village schools are closed for the sake of economy, this is money ill-saved, if the fundamental basis for the future of the children (including even their temperamental willingness and ability to learn in the future) is to be sacrificed.

If small schools are closed because their facilities are below the standard demanded, their classrooms too small or their lavatories too few, then it seems once again that local authorities must be required to think what they actually value most, what schools are actually *for*. To close a school which fulfils its function well, in which children are being educated with the right aims in view and successfully, by these standards, on the grounds of some technical fault in the physical environment must be wrong. Parents and managers must continue to press, as they do now, for the saving of any school which, by educational criteria, is a good school. High on the list of educational criteria to be applied must come the moral atmosphere of the school.

In the case of secondary schools, if it is argued that they must be large in order to be able to generate a sixth form large enough for a full range of A level subjects to be on offer (the commonest argument for large comprehensive schools) then this argument in turn must be defeated. Choice of subject is not in itself the most important value; it is far better, as I have argued already, that a few subjects should be well taught than that the whole range of possible choices should be available. And if a pupil cannot do the subject he wants, then let him transfer to a school where he can. Some system of sharing of sixth forms will be necessary as school rolls decrease in order to keep the actual number of schools from being radically reduced. Let no one think that 'rationalization' can be carried out without disastrous effects, not so much on the academic as on the moral education of children.

The future must be seen in terms of numbers of small comprehensive schools, towards which both pupils and teachers can feel a sense of commitment, and whose ideals and standards can be felt to be coherent and consistent. Just as society has had to rethink the apparent logic of high-rise housing, because of its dehumanizing effect, so society is having to go back on the arguments in favour of vast schools. Academic arguments are not the only ones appropriate to determine the size of a school, nor will economic arguments alone suffice. In addition, one has to consider what it is like to be a member of any school. And there is no doubt that good schools are, to a certain extent, necessarily *cosy*. Certainly all the requirements for the moral education of children depend upon its element of intimacy, and cannot be met without it.

One may ask to what extent a school is responsible for the behaviour of its pupils outside school itself. So far most of the discussion has centred on morality *in* school. What education should children be given about how to behave in the world at large? An answer to this question has been suggested already, in that if the early moral education of a child has been successful, if he has become gradually morally aware and has begun to acquire virtues of character, then these virtues and this awareness will be manifest out of school as well as in school. Honesty, a dislike of violence, an ability to keep promises and commitments—these virtues will inevitably affect a child's behaviour in the ordinary transactions of his life, as well as his behaviour in school.

To take an example: one of the problems of behaviour most urgently in need of solution in society is that of vandalism. School itself may provide what is lacking at home, namely a sense of pride in and protectiveness of personal possessions, and thus, by analogy, a respect for other people's possessions. Some schools for the maladjusted, for instance, immediately institute a private area for each pupil, as soon as he arrives, and insist that he keep there his *own* books, pens, postcards, whatever else he has, insist too that he look after them. The sense of impersonality, the feeling that no particular, real person cares about something or owns it, is an evil in society. It can be mitigated at school, if special attention is accorded to this problem.

At least it is obvious that a school must, and must be known to, side with the law. So where a pupil has broken the law, the school will cooperate with the police and the probation service as best it can, though always with the interest of the pupil in mind. It is extremely useful if a school can make this general stance clear, before any specific case arises in a particular group of children, so that pupils and parents may know what kind of reaction to expect from the school.

With regard to sexual morality, however, an area within which both schools and parents tend to blame each other, the case is more difficult. Undoubtedly most parents want a school to provide sex education. It must be provided early, and perhaps over a considerable number of years. I believe that it should take a more or less standard form, at least within each local authority area, and if it is partly provided by means of films or television programmes, then parents can find out for themselves what the basis of the education is going to be. This seems to be a great advantage. But apart from a legitimate emphasis on the risks of pregnancy and venereal disease, it is probably inappropriate for such instruction to be particularly moralistic in tone. In whatever way parents or schools wish that children should behave sexually, it is extremely unlikely that when the question actually arises for the individual he is likely to be at all influenced by the moral precepts of others. This is so particularly if the precepts come from school, thought to be notoriously old fashioned, if not blankly ignorant, in matters concerned with the relations between the sexes. In matters which so closely affect the personal life of its pupils, and yet do not fall within the powers of the law, it is necessary for a school to exercise both tact and discretion, and a respect for privacy. If it does not, then all the good which may have been built up over the years in the way of mutual respect and trust between teacher and pupil will be suddenly and irrevocably undone. A school may rightly claim to have a concern with the question whether or not its pupils are going in for criminal activities. It is on far more shaky ground where no criminal charges are in question.

It is not only in the case of sexual morality that such tact has to be exercised. The relations between a child and his parents may force equally difficult decisions on the school about what line, even what 'side', to take. I do not believe that there are any useful general rules that can be laid down here. The only guide is that the school must try to do everything it can to help the pupil to progress steadily towards the goals of education. There is much to be said, in the case of adolescents, for keeping these goals quite explicitly in view. Then only if the pupil's private life is quite manifestly constituting an obstacle to their attainment should the question of discussing, and perhaps reforming it, be allowed to arise. In any case advice is more appropriate than admonition or command, and then only if sought.

Moral education is, then, an important aspect, some might think the most important aspect, of education at school. Like all education it has as its aim the improvement of the life that a child will live after he has left school. He should be better off, in this case a better kind of person, than he would have been if he had never been to school. Moral education will have been successful only if the child, and society as a whole, benefits in this way. If the general ethos and pressures of school life have actually made him worse, if he has acquired no virtues and only certain vices from his teachers and his contemporaries, then his school must be deemed a bad school, even if the rest of his education has been efficient.

I have argued that 'moral lessons', with a syllabus consisting of the discussion and analysis of hypothetical problems and their solutions, or of actual social problems, have their place, and may be valuable and stimulating. But these lessons will go no way at all towards constituting moral education in the only serious sense, that of making children morally better. This has to be done by means of the example, the interventions and the consistent and deliberate moral policy of the teachers in the school. Consistency is of the greatest importance. This is perhaps partly why it is often held that Catholic schools are best at moral education. In Catholic schools there tends to be a presumption, not only of interest in matters of morality but of a shared *standard* of morality, confidently proclaimed. Vacillation and loss of nerve may be less conspicuous among the staff, especially nuns and priests. Whether this reputation is deserved or not, it is certain that a great diversity of moral standards is confusing for a child; and that lack of interest in morality, or extremes of timidity in the making of moral judgements, are totally disastrous for moral education. What is needed is an explicit policy in every school, and a full recognition by the teachers themselves that the teaching of good behaviour in its widest sense is as much part of their task as the teaching of their particular subject: that this does not mean simply taking on an occasional supervisory duty, but rather providing for the pupils in the school a constant reminder that there are ways of doing things which are good, and others which are bad.

Heads of schools, above all, have a tremendous responsibility for this aspect of education, and in any school in which the head has lost his nerve, or is unsure of his commitment to a standard of morality, the moral education of the pupils is likely effectively to come to an end. In the selection of staff, for one thing, a head has great influence. But he can also make it clear to those working with him that they create the general ethos of the school, and he must watch for signs of things going wrong. He must trust the staff who manifestly make things go right, even if in unexpected and imaginative ways. It is a matter for despair when one hears of heads who make an enormous issue of what clothes the women teachers wear, and yet are too timid to ensure that teachers mark work conscientiously, keep promises to children, or refrain from victimizing children who are irritating or unattractive.

A good head should be brave enough to state clearly and in moral terms what he expects his staff to do, the influence that he recognizes they will have. He should himself be prepared to set the standards which he wants upheld in every aspect of school life. It is, as I have said, a great responsibility; and there is a further point. The best head in the world depends upon good teachers if his school is to be a good school. How are good teachers to be found? Is it possible to make them, or are they born? No educational needs of any kind can be met except by teachers fit to meet them. It is to the training of such teachers that we now must turn.

Teachers

Good schools depend on good teachers. So much would be agreed. But to agree with such platitudes is not enough. In trying to look towards a satisfactory future for education in this country, there is nowhere in which action is more urgently needed than in the reform of teacher training.

At present, teacher training falls into various rather different traps. Sometimes it is committed to an old-fashioned snobbishness, a desire to demonstrate that teachers, too, are interested in particular academic disciplines and can be as pure as the purest professor. Sometimes the trainers of teachers are devoted to theory to the extent of being indifferent to or ignorant of the school itself, and what it does. This remoteness may, again, originate in a kind of snobbishness. There has to be a theory or a philosophy of education if the study and the practice of education is to be as respectable and as professional as other studies and pursuits. Sometimes the training of teachers, on the other hand, is all too practical: teachers are led to believe that they have a unique opportunity for changing the views of their pupils, for turning them into critics or subverters of society, and that this opportunity must in no circumstances be thrown away. In all these ways the training of teachers may be deflected from the central task, which is the consideration of children's educational needs, and how to satisfy them. There is far too little emphasis on the actual manner in which a curriculum may start to meet these needs, or on how the needs should be identified in the real classroom setting. So much would, I think, be pretty generally agreed.

But teacher training is a field in which action is hard to take. Teachers themselves are jealous of outside interference with their profession. Aspiring to the professional status of doctors or lawyers, they believe that they should be allowed to establish their own professional standards. Yet they lack the esoteric knowledge of doctors or lawyers, the almost mysterious expertise which seems to set those professions above lay criticism or interference. On the other hand, because the future of their children is not directly affected by the way teachers are trained, as it is by, for example, the closure of schools, or the abolishing of selection, parents are not likely to form pressure groups or demand reform. Nor is the reform of teacher training a vote-catching enterprise for any political party. Nevertheless it is of the utmost urgency, and any plan for the future of education must essentially incorporate a plan for the teachers.

One preliminary point must be made: whatever reforms are agreed, either in the structure or the content of initial teacher training, it is no use relying on these alone if the competence (and hence the reputation in society at large) of the teaching profession is to be improved in the foreseeable future. For if initial training were changed immediately it would take twenty or thirty years for the whole staff of all schools to benefit from this. And although a new spirit might gradually creep through the schools it would take a long time to become effective. Of course things are not quite as dramatic as that, nor as clear-cut. For one thing, there are already many excellent and enlightened teachers in schools who had very inadequate training or none at all. Moreover, it has to be remembered that training alone, however excellent, will not make a bad teacher a good one. All the same, it is necessary that any new scheme should envisage a sharp and immediate injection of in-service training so that those teachers already in post could benefit from the new ideas.

There is in any case a good argument for in-service training, apart from the somewhat short term and negative argument outlined above. Teachers ought to have the opportunity while they are actually in post of using their experience to build up further specialization. There is everything to be said for having them pay for their own courses, possibly borrowing money from local authorities to do so, provided that on acquiring a further qualification, they would get a related increase in salary. In this way, like doctors, they could improve their own career prospects and benefit the profession as a whole by progressively acquainting themselves with new ideas and new expertise.

Even if in-service courses could be taken part-time, and over a longish period, and even if teachers paid for their own attendance on the courses, they would still be expensive for local authorities, who would have to pay lecturers or advisory teachers to teach on the courses, and provide substitutes for those teachers who were attending full or part-time. Ever since 1972, when the James Committee on the training of teachers gave top priority to in-service training, which was the third cycle of training envisaged for every teacher, local authorities have been evading their responsibilities to pay for such courses. Something is being done, it is true, but not enough. In 1978, after a threat from the Secretary of State that earmarked money might have to be used, a gentleman's agreement was reached between the Department and the local authorities as to how much should be spent on in-service training. By halfway through the year it had become clear that local authorities had broken this agreement, and spent a million pounds less than was promised. It is fairly evident that only earmarked grants specifically for such training will actually bring results.

If in-service training could be seriously considered as part of a teacher's course then there could be a pattern of training suitable both for specialized and general needs. Ideally, initial training should last for four years. It would include a three-year degree course which might, but need not, include some educational element, a general highly practical year after that, which would allow a teacher to be licensed to teach; and a period of in-service training for the full certificate. There could be a wide choice of different in-service courses for this last part, specializing in, say, the teaching of modern languages with a view to speaking the language, the teaching of advanced mathematics to gifted children, the teaching of English to slow learners, the teaching of maladjusted or disruptive children, and many more. At the end of the first three years, a potential teacher would have to decide to specialize in the pre-fourteen or post-fourteen age group, but though his professional year would be concentrated according to this choice, there is no reason in principle why a teacher trained for one sort of teaching should not move on to another.

In this way one could envisage a flexible, competent and professionally expert teaching force. Uniformity of standards, if not of course-content, should be aimed at, by means of a system of external examination and a monitoring system like that operated at present by the CNAA with regard to degree courses in polytechnics. There should be far greater use made of senior practising teachers in the training process, and somehow the present jealousy and suspicion often found between College of Education staff and teachers should be brought to an end. This might indeed come about if teachers came to regard the training of beginners as perhaps the most serious part of their task, for which they need the utmost cooperation with universities, polytechnics and colleges of higher education, and if the staffs of those institutions came to realize the benefit of practical experience. Much more interchange between the two should take place.

But it may be thought that this is an unduly optimistic picture of the future state of the profession. Even if it is not, it may well be objected that to talk of the general structure of the training system is futile unless one is first clear about what potential teachers need to learn. What is the content of this long-drawn-out training actually to be? In the light of the preceding chapters, in which I have attempted to lay down the necessary conditions for a school to be a good school, namely that it should satisfy the educational needs of its students, it is now possible to state quite briefly what prospective teachers ought to learn, in order to bring such schools into reality.

In the first place, if the common curriculum is crucial, if it must be constructed with the future benefits of the children in mind, then it is essential that teachers should believe in it and should primarily learn to teach what is central to this curriculum. They must learn how to promote the essential literacy, numeracy and technical competence which are to form the central compulsory core of the school programme. Not all teachers will, obviously, teach all of these subjects, except possibly to the youngest children. But the essential thing is that no one should teach them who is not professionally competent to do so.

And believing in this curriculum means not only seeing the point of it, but realizing that in teaching it there are criteria of success and failure. Teachers must become more professional, more conscious of the merits and demerits of their own performance. They must be prepared to use standards of successful teaching, by means of records and tests and other monitoring techniques, so that they can demonstrate to parents, governors and local authority advisors that they are not only teaching the necessary things, but teaching them well. Many teachers now have the feeling that they can do what they like, that they can have total command over their own classes and are answerable to no one outside; this must be eliminated. With the introduction of a curriculum based firmly on the needs of the child, with respect to his life outside school, criteria of good teaching brought in and applied by the outside world must necessarily be accepted by the profession. The isolation of the teacher in a school-bounded world, with standards understood only by himself, must be brought to an end.

A teacher, then, must learn the techniques of teaching some of the compulsory curriculum subjects, and of estimating his own performance in teaching them. Alternatively, if he is going to teach at secondary school he may concentrate on the techniques of teaching his own specialist university subject. But more teachers should in addition be prepared to take part in the teaching of roughly speaking 'current affairs' or social studies. More should be ready to teach both the practical matters of everyday life, and perhaps the history, geography and economics of the locality where they teach, even if this means 'getting it up' with regard to each school. If there are to be such lessons on the timetable of all children, at least until they are fourteen, then the more different people who teach them the better. For different interests and different points of view will serve to bring realism and interest to what should be highly realistic and intelligible, indeed 'relevant' lessons.

Thirdly, if a teacher is to make the best possible use of

material from different sources, he must be able and willing to use broadcast or taped programmes. It is therefore absolutely essential that he be competent to use video cassettes as well as television, and should be able to tape his own material when he wants to. At present a great deal of potentially useful equipment sits about on shelves at school because teachers are too ignorant to use it. They are frightened of their own incompetence. If the machines go wrong they have no idea what to do next. And their clumsiness and lack of understanding make it inevitable that the machines will go wrong. An elementary competence in the use of electronic equipment then is an essential part of the training of all teachers.

Finally, and perhaps most important of all, a teacher must learn how to recognize the particular different needs of the children in his class. I have argued that it is only if teachers are prepared to 'set' children at school, to divide them according to ability in different subjects, and to appreciate when a child needs to be taken out of a regular class and given extra or different teaching, that the comprehensive ideal of a good education for all children can be approached. The success of the whole educational enterprise, then, turns on the willingness and the ability of teachers to detect the particular educational needs of children, to pick up early signs of frustration of failure, of falling behind or of serious inability to learn alongside other children, for whatever reason.

To be ready to pick up such signs does not mean that every teacher needs to be expert in all the different kinds of handicap or disadvantage, sensory or psychological, that a child may have. It is rather that he must *expect* children to have special needs, and must know where to turn, for specialist help and advice. He must be able to set the wheels in motion for a proper expert assessment of a child's needs, and that at an early stage.

This demands confidence on the part of the teacher. And this is the respect in which training will help him. It is very easy for a teacher, especially if young and relatively inexperienced to think that a disruptive child or one who persistently fails, is a matter of blame for the teacher. A child's failure is translated into a teacher's failure and then pride forbids the seeking of outside help. Such an attitude is disastrous both for the child and the teacher. At least part of the professional training of teachers must be devoted to learning to seek help, learning exactly to describe the signs which point to a problem, and learning that it is the teacher's first duty to ensure that children's needs are assessed. And these needs of course include the need for advanced teaching, more mathematics, a new language, specialist music lessons, just as much as the need for a hearing aid, or for remedial reading lessons.

As a means to forming a rational judgement about children, teachers must be shown how to keep good, clear records of the progress of members of their class. They must be efficient in the administering of tests, and in the writing of reports. Moreover they must be made aware of the difficult problems of confidentiality which will arise for them in the course of their careers, and they must be taught to consult with, and listen to, the parents of the children they teach.

In addition a teacher needs to learn how to manage a class (and this includes the detection of special needs already referred to). Colleges of education must use micro-teaching techniques (the detailed analysis and criticism of actual parts of lessons, video-recorded and played back). Other techniques, such as simulated teaching, can be used in the colleges themselves without necessarily going into actual class rooms. Obviously some actual teaching practice is also needed. But it would be impossible for all the professional skills a teacher needs to be acquired in this way. For one thing, the schools themselves could not accommodate enough student teachers for long enough periods without disastrous effects. But whatever the methods used, what the new training amounts to is the inculcation of a new professionalism, and a new attitude to teaching.

Standards must be high. The professional part of the teacher's course should no longer be the semi-automatic thing it sometimes is now. It should be possible to fail it; indeed it should be difficult to pass. This would be no hardship, if it always came as a fourth year, after a full degree course, in whatever subject. For the failed teacher would still have a degree, as well as some useful, if painful, experience. The standing of the teaching profession itself meanwhile would be enormously improved if it were seen that it was a profession with its own high standards.

These are heavy demands. To train teachers in this way will not necessarily take more time than the present training. There is a good deal in the present courses, the vaguely historical and philosophical elements, the theory of education, which could very well be omitted to make room for the new and more rigorous professional content.

But however excellent a programme of training may be, there will always remain the deep-seated objection that good teachers are born, not made. Nature's teachers can manage without training. Others will never be able to teach, whatever help they get. It is difficult to assess the true weight of this objection. The myth of the great natural teacher is one which will always flourish. For nearly everyone is fortunate enough to remember at least one brilliant teacher from his school days, and such teachers tend, in memory at least, to be full of character, idiosyncratic to the point of eccentricity, dogmatic, intuitive, with a high disregard for rules. In addition many of them were, and are, brilliant teachers because they were funny, they could actually make people laugh. To describe such a person is, obviously to describe precisely someone who could not be 'produced' by any kind of education or training. I do not want to attempt to explode the myth of the natural teacher. But there are two points to bear in mind. First, at least part of the professional training described above is concerned with the learning of skills (such as the skill of working a tape-recorder) which could in no way inhibit 'naturalness' but which cannot on the other hand just be picked up without training. Secondly, the good teacher is very like, in some deep way akin to, the good actor. And though it is true that some people can act and others cannot, by nature, yet no one denies the need for actors to be trained. I believe that, by analogy, even a 'born' teacher will be improved by training and cannot get on without it; while one who is not 'born', may nevertheless, by hard work, be made reasonably competent. And a school full of dazzling eccentrics and prima donnas would after all be difficult to bear. Some of the more modest teachers are absolutely essential, as long as they too have acquired the skills which can be taught them.

Improvement in training is crucial if there is to be any improvement of the education service as a whole; but it is very difficult to foresee any action as long as the powers of initiation remain as they are. Neither central nor local government have any strong motive to act, and the universities are, on the whole, uninterested in reform, or, if they are interested, can be effective only piecemeal.

The report of the James Committee, concerned, in any case, almost entirely with the structure and not the content of teacher training, had practically no effect after its publication in 1972. There is no point in demanding another report. What is needed is a central policy, put into practice by a body with actual powers to inspect, monitor and examine (or at least to nominate its own external examiners to college-based examining boards). Either the teaching profession itself in partnership with the Department of Education and Science, or an independent body, such as the Council for National Academic Awards, should provide the central initiative, lay down the requirements of certification, and ensure that the in-service elements of training were actually systematically supplied before any teacher could be certificated.

For the comprehensive ideal, discussed and defended (with certain provisos) in chapter 3, demands for its success a special kind of teacher of whom we have far too few. Those teachers who are good, indeed excellent, are good in spite of their training, or so it often appears. It is futile for any government or local authority to demand a kind of educational system which must rely to an overwhelming extent on high professionalism and educated judgement on the part of teachers, and then show indifference to the actual training of those teachers.

It is not surprising if often we are told that comprehensive education has failed. No one has seriously tried to ensure that a new kind of teacher should match a new kind of school. What is needed is a teacher who is both capable of understanding and demanding a high standard in the particular subject he teaches, and is genuinely well-informed and competent in matters of everyday life in society. And, most important of all, we need teachers who have confidence in their own values. They must be able to distinguish pupils' educational needs, and to make moral demands of the pupils, with firmness and clarity of judgement. For any political party to proclaim an interest in education while showing no practical interest in the professional requirements of those who provide it is a manifest contradiction.

*   *   *

None of the ideas put forward in the preceding chapters is at all revolutionary. On the contrary, since education is an element of society as it is: since, in part at least, it is concerned with a system of knowledge and understanding which has its roots in history, educational thinking must be conservative. You must understand what there is, before setting about to change it. Conservatism in this sense is not the prerogative of any one political party.

However, there is another sense in which education, if it fulfils the needs of children as they were outlined at the beginning, is anti-conservative in nature. For of all the educational needs a child has, if he is to live a good life after he has left school, perhaps the most important is the need to develop his imagination. It is by means of his imagination that he can interest himself in the world (including of course the worlds of art, music and literature), and can envisage a future, perhaps radically different from the present, which he may do something to bring about. It is certainly one of the main functions of education to produce such a critical awareness of the present, and of how it might be changed. Ignorance constitutes bondage: the better educated a man is, the more free, and the more capable of independent action.

A common curriculum shared in its general goals by all children is in no way inimical to individual imaginative growth. It is because children (and their teachers) are all members of one society that we can identify certain shared educational needs. The common curriculum must be judged according to how well it satisfies them. But one of the common goals must be that of independence; and this means not only the ability to earn a living and be self supporting, but also to be critical and willing, if necessary, to reject the assumptions of one's fellows.

Nevertheless education is not possible if no one has, or no one expresses *any* convictions; or if nothing is thought to be either true or false, either good or bad, either a matter of importance or of indifference. A teacher who is genuinely neutral, or who thinks it is his duty to pretend to a neutrality he does not have, is depriving his pupils, not so much of specific guidance, as of the example of someone who has feelings and convictions, who can distinguish things that differ, and will act on his beliefs. And that is a genuine deprivation. Perhaps the most destructive force in education in the past two decades has been the growth of a relativism which has infected both academic teaching and the teaching of morality. To avoid relativism takes nerve; and a failure of nerve among teachers may account for much that has been bad about education since the war.

There will, of course, always be good and bad schools. No system of education can eliminate all bad teachers, nor can education alone cure all the social ills of the world, or by itself prevail against all the other factors in society which may influence a child for ill rather than good. Nevertheless, schools in which a clear curricular aim is known to exist, in which a standard of performance and of behaviour is known to be demanded, in which parents may, if they want to, discuss with teachers what the goals of the school are and how well their own children are progressing towards these goals . . . such schools are more likely to succeed than any others. Moreover, a system in which it is taken for granted that children have different needs, different abilities and different obstacles to overcome in their course towards the agreed educational ends is far more likely to engender confidence, both in parents and in children themselves, than a system in which it is pretended that everyone is the same.

Perhaps, after all, explicitly to state the goals of education, to assert the values of competence, independence, imagination and morality, and to be prepared to judge education in schools according to these values, is after all to propose a view which in some sense is revolutionary. At least it would overturn the commonly stated proposition that education is not a matter of politics. Instead it would insist that, being a question of values and of public policy, education is completely political. But, therefore, it is something in which society as a whole has a legitimate interest. If, as I have argued, it is proper to ask the question *What is education for?* then the answer must be in terms of values, on which society is prepared not only to spend its money, but also to stake its future.

Index

Adulthood, preparation for, 3–10, 18–35 *passim*, 36, 47, 65, 101–3

Assessment, 67–75; 'descriptive', 69–70; structure of, 70–5 *see also* Examination system

Associated board of language schools, 42

Careers, 5–6

Catholic school education, 90–1

Childhood, *see* Preschool education

CNAA, 95

Colleges of education, 95, 98

Comprehensive, the, 9, 36–54, 55, 87; choice of subjects within, 52–4, 87; curriculum in, 40–54, 70, 76–91 *passim*, 95–103 *passim*; educational needs and, 36–54 *passim*; examination system in, 41–2, 46, 49–53, 70–5; 'gifted' children in, 55–66; ideals of, 37–54 *passim*, 55, 97, 100; language teaching in, 40–3; mixed-ability in, 43–52, 66, 67–75; moral education in, 76–91, 102–3; principle of selection in, 41–54; social class and, 37, 58, 64–6

Compulsory education, 1, 3, 11–12

Control, education as, 22–6

Curriculum; common, 18–35, 36, 40–1, 46–7, 70, 95–103 *passim*; the 'comprehensive, 40–54, 70, 76–91 *passim*, 95–103 *passim*; compulsory and optional subjects in, 32–3, 46–54, 74; concept of, 19–20; 'hidden', 6, 82–91 *passim*; mixed-ability, 43–52, 66, 67–75; moral education in the, 76–91; 102–3; organization of the, 29–35; 'purist' view of, 21–6; subject-dominated, 27–35; teachers and the, 20–1, 27–35 *passim*, 95–103

Eavis, P., 40

Education, provision of, 1, 20; for the 'gifted' child, 55–66; preschool, 11–13, 15–17, 18

Education Act (1944), the, 22

Equality, educational, 8–10, 37–8, 43, 65

Eleven-plus, the, 8, 37, 41, 72

Elitism, 37

Examination system, the, 28, 32–3, 41–2, 46, 59–53; 'A' level, 46, 52, 53–4, 73–5; 'B' level, 71–5; CSE, 50–1, 72–5; debates about, 67–70; 'O' level, 49–53, 71–5; in primary